TEACHER EDITION

7

Family Life

David Thomas, PhD

General Editor

RCL
Benziger®

Allen, Texas

Consultants

Paul Duckro, PhD
Tim Hogan, PsyD
Tom Everson
Fanny Pedraza

RCL Benziger Development Team

James Spurgin
Editor

Tricia Legault
Design

Laura Fremder
Production

Daniel S. Mulhall
National Catechetical Advisor

Jo Rotunno
Director of Catechist and Professional Development

Susan Smith
Director of Project Development

Ed DeStefano
Publisher

Peter M. Esposito
President

NIHIL OBSTAT
Rev. Msgr. Robert Coerver
Censor Librorum

IMPRIMATUR
† Most Reverend Kevin J. Farrell DD
Bishop of Dallas

May 3, 2010

The *Nihil Obstat* and *Imprimatur* are official declarations that the material reviewed is free of doctrinal or moral error. No implication is contained therein that those granting the *Nihil Obstat* and *Imprimatur* agree with the contents, opinions, or statements expressed.

Send all inquiries to:
RCL Benziger   Toll Free   877-275-4725
206 East Bethany Drive   Fax   800-688-8356
Allen, TX 75002-3804

Visit us at www.RCLBenziger.com

20657   ISBN 978-0-7829-1507-5 (Student Edition)
20667   ISBN 978-0-7829-1517-4 (Parent Connection)
20687   ISBN 978-0-7829-1537-2 (Teacher Edition)

2nd printing.
Manufactured for RCL Benziger in Cincinnati, OH, USA. October 2010.

ACKNOWLEDGMENTS

Excerpts from Guidelines for *Programs to Reduce Child Victimization* provided courtesy of The National Center for Missing and Exploited Children.

Excerpts from the *National Directory for Catechesis* © 2005, United States Conference of Catholic Bishops, Washington, D.C. Excerpts from the *Charter for the Protection of Children and Young People* © 2006, United States Conference of Catholic Bishops, Washington, D.C. Excerpts from the *Catechetical Formation in Chaste Living: Guidelines for Curriculum Design and Publication* © 2008, United States Conference of Catholic Bishops, Washington, D.C. Excerpts from *Human Sexuality: A Catholic Perspective for Education and Lifelong Learning* © 1991, United States Catholic Conference, Inc. Washington, D.C. Excerpts from *Human Life in Our Day* © 1968, United States Conference of Catholic Bishops, Washington, D.C. Excerpts from the *New American Bible* with Revised New Testament and Revised Psalms © 1991, 1986, 1970 Confraternity of Christian Doctrine, Washington, D.C. and are used by permission of the copyright owner. All Rights Reserved. No part of the New American Bible may be reproduced in any form without permission in writing from the copyright owner.

Excerpts from Benedict XVI, Encyclical Letter, *Deus Caritas Est* (25 December 2005). Excerpts from Benedict XVI, Encyclical Letter, *Caritas in Veritate* (29 June 2009). Excerpts from the Pontifical Council for the Family, *The Truth and Meaning of Human Sexuality* (8 December 1995). Excerpts from Second Vatican Council, Pastoral Constitution on the Church in the Modern World, *Gaudium et Spes* (7 December 1965). Excerpts from John Paul II, General Audience, *Original Unity of Man and Woman* (16 January 1980). Excerpts from John Paul II, Apostolic Exhortation, *Familiaris Consortio* (22 November 1981). Excerpts from the English translation of the *Catechism of the Catholic Church* © 1994, 1997, United States Conference of Catholic Bishops. Libreria Editrice Vaticana. Used with permission. All rights reserved.

CONTENTS

Program Overview

Welcome to RCL Benziger *Family Life* 4
QuickStart for Teachers and Catechists 12
Models for Implementation 28
Scope and Sequence for Grade 7 29

Unit 1: God's Gift of Family

Unit Background 30
Lesson 1: Family Relationships 32
Lesson 2: Values and Virtues 38
Reviewing Unit 1 44

Unit 2: God's Gift of Self

Unit Background 46
Lesson 3: Identity 48
Lesson 4: Gender 54
Reviewing Unit 2 60

Unit 3: God's Gift of Life

Unit Background 62
Lesson 5: Wellness 64
Lesson 6: Choose Life 70
Reviewing Unit 3 76

Unit 4: God's Gift of Love

Unit Background 78
Lesson 7: Love Is 80
Lesson 8: Chastity 86
Reviewing Unit 4 92

Unit 5: God's Gift of Community

Unit Background 94
Lesson 9: Consequences 96
Lesson 10: Civility 102
Reviewing Unit 5 108

Additional Resources

Reviewing This Year 110
Glossary 114

A comprehensive moral catechesis for families with children in grades K–8

RCL Benziger *Family Life* offers unparalleled support for Catholic families. This unique series:

- ▸ presents skills and virtues for Catholic family living.

- ▸ places human sexuality within the context of Catholic family moral living.

- ▸ helps families address the complex issues of contemporary life.

New! ▸ offers in-depth support for child safety education.

- ▸ provides solid support for Spanish-speaking families reflecting the unique gifts and challenges of Latino cultures.

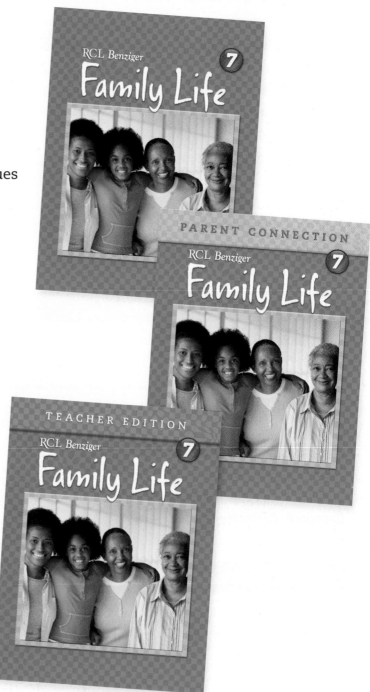

Three Key Components for Each Grade Level

Three key components (Student Edition, Teacher Edition and Parent Connection) provide resources for parents, children, religion teachers and catechists to explore, reflect on and decide ways to integrate into their lives each year on five themes in Catholic family living:

- ▸ God's Gift of Family

- ▸ God's Gift of Self

- ▸ God's Gift of Life

- ▸ God's Gift of Love

- ▸ God's Gift of Community

Student Edition, Parent Connection, Teacher Edition

Additional Resources

Human Reproduction Booklets for Grades 5 and 6

Level A: The Reproductive System and Procreation

Level B: New Life in the Womb and The Miracle of Birth

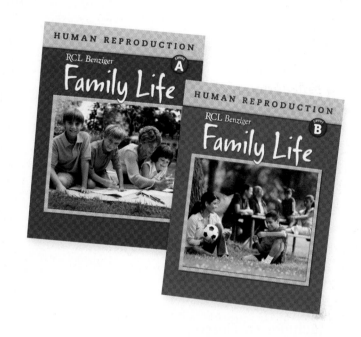

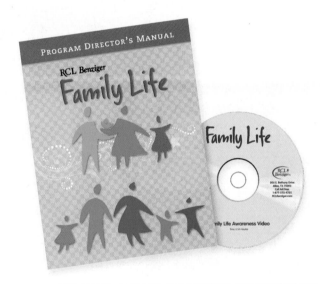

Support for Program Directors

▶ Program Director's Manual

▶ DVD in-service video

▶ Ongoing web support at RCLBFamilyLife.com

In-service DVD

The RCL Benziger *Family Life* DVD contains a video overview of the program and separate in-service segments for teachers, catechists and parents.

Resources for Spanish-speaking Parents

▶ Parent booklet

▶ Parent letters for each unit

▶ Two-page Family Time resource for each unit

Student Edition

RCL Benziger *Family Life* Student Edition guides the child and their family through a reflection on each year's curriculum.

Family Time

Each unit begins with a two-page Family Time feature. This NEW feature enables the family and the class to focus on the same themes during the two lessons that make up each unit.

Student Lesson

Each unit includes two lessons. Each lesson has three simple parts: **Engage, Teach,** and **Apply.**

Engage: An opening page engages the student, activates their prior knowledge, and grounds the lesson content in the young person's experience.

Teach: Lesson presentation develops unit theme and highlights vocabulary words

Catholics Believe summarizes the main point of the lesson.

Growing in Virtue highlights the lesson virtue that strengthens the student and family to live a holy and healthy family life.

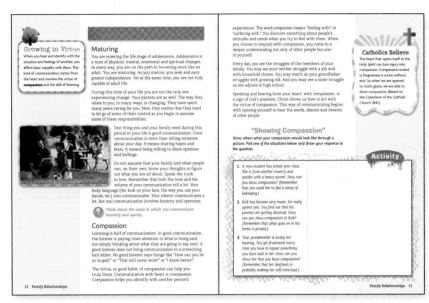

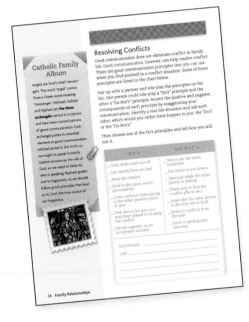

Apply: Concluding activity integrates lesson content and invites a faith choice.

Catholic Family Album highlights a saint or holy person or Catholic organization that exemplifies the lesson theme.

Additional Student Edition Features

▶ The Catholic Home
  (Includes Catholic prayers and practices)

▶ Unit reviews

▶ End-of-the-year review

▶ Certificate to recognize achievement

Teacher Edition

Your RCL Benziger *Family Life* Teacher Edition offers you comprehensive support including these innovative features:

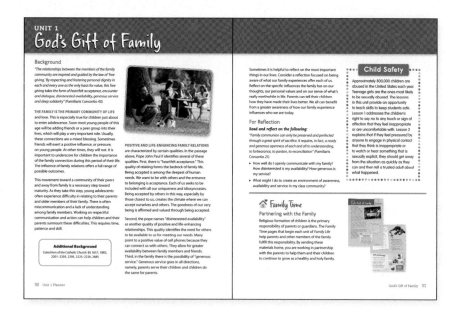

Unit Background Pages

A theological and catechetical background essay puts you at ease.

Lesson Planner

A practical lesson planner for each of the ten lessons forecasts everything you will need.

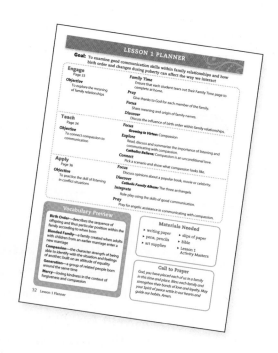

Wraparound Lesson Plans

Creative lesson plans offer you a simple core plan plus teaching tips and ideas for enriching the lessons.

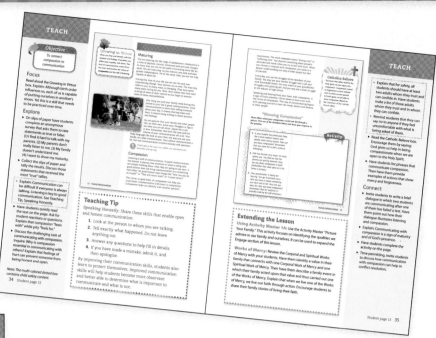

Child Safety

The program integrates key concepts of child safety education across the nine grade levels, Kindergarten through Grade 8.

▶ A child safety unit preview is included on the background page.

▶ Content related to child safety education is highlighted within the lesson plans.

Activities, Reviews and Glossary

Additional resources are available, such as a cumulative glossary of family life vocabulary words found in the back of your Teacher Edition.

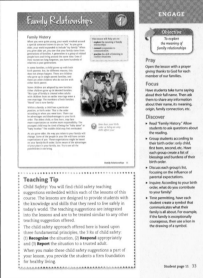

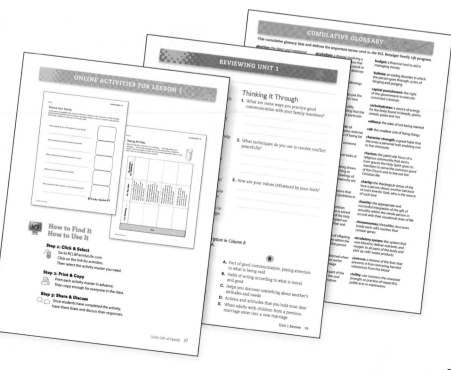

Parent Connection

The Parent Connection magazine supports the parents' role as the first and primary educators of their children in faith and moral living. The magazine provides:

- a moral catechesis for family living related to the lesson themes in the student book.

- practical strategies for communicating and working together as a household of faith.

- tips for discussing difficult issues with young people.

- a glossary of terms taught in the program, according to grade level.

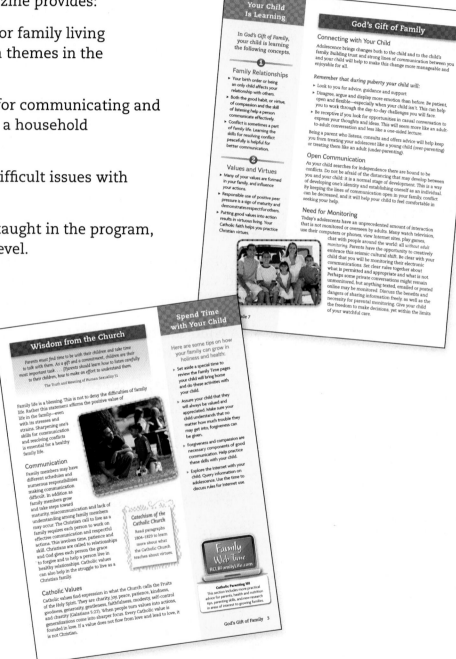

Additional Components

RCL Benziger *Family Life* offers comprehensive support for the program coordinator.

Program Director's Manual

This comprehensive manual offers a wealth of features to support the program coordinator, teachers, catechists, and parents. All pages are reproducible. Highlights include:

- ▶ overview of program
- ▶ models for in-service sessions for parents and teachers/catechists
- ▶ handouts for in-service sessions
- ▶ professional articles
- ▶ English and Spanish versions of parent letters
- ▶ Spanish translations of all Family Time pages
- ▶ scope and sequence chart for entire program
- ▶ glossary of key terms and themes
- ▶ index of key issues taught throughout the program

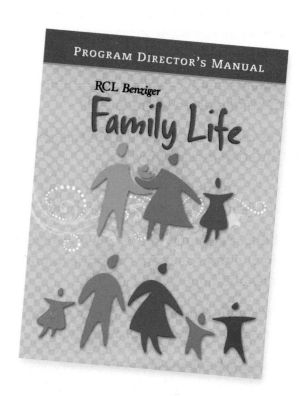

QuickStart Workshop

A practical video-assisted workshop prepares you for your role in family life education.

RCL Benziger

Family Life

Web Site

Web support for the program includes a variety of resources for program coordinators, teachers, catechists, students, and parents as well as a discussion group that allows networking with other users of RCL Benziger *Family Life*.

Introduction

From its inception, RCL Benziger *Family Life* has remained faithful to the enduring vision of assisting the family through resources that help it grow as the domestic Church. RCL Benziger *Family Life*:

▸ provides a moral catechesis for children from kindergarten to grade eight.

▸ places human sexuality within the context of Christian moral living.

▸ offers a catechesis of hope against the challenges facing the Catholic family.

▸ introduces children to the joys of virtuous living and teaches them the skills to grow healthy and holy.

▸ teaches children the skills they need to make good decisions to protect them from harm.

▸ adapts to the changing times and needs of the Church with each new edition.

RCL Benziger *Family Life* is designed to prepare young people to live safe and healthy, moral and loving lives as members of the Christian family. The series provides a catechesis for moral living focusing at each grade level on the five themes of:

▸ God's Gift of Family

▸ God's Gift of Self

▸ God's Gift of Life

▸ God's Gift of Love

▸ God's of Community

Why a New Edition of RCL Benziger *Family Life*?

In 2002 the U.S. Conference of Catholic Bishops approved the groundbreaking *Charter for the Protection of Children*. In the Charter the bishops committed the Catholic Church in the United States to "creating a safe environment within the Church for children and youth" (Preamble).

In Article 12 of the Charter, the bishops commit the Church in the United States to "maintain 'safe environment' programs" in accord with Catholic moral principles conducted cooperatively with parents to provide education and training for children.

This edition of RCL Benziger *Family Life* has been revised to assist parishes and dioceses to provide this safe environment training to the Church's children and youth, and to provide support to their parents and teachers who are responsible for their education and safety. RCL Benziger *Family Life* has been revised in consultation with the USCCB Secretariat for Child and Youth Protection, building upon the child safety guidelines developed by numerous (arch) dioceses, and fully incorporating the USCCB 2007 document *Catechetical Formation in Chaste Living: Guidelines for Curriculum Design and Publication*.

The student and teacher materials in the RCL Benziger *Family Life* series have been reviewed by the USCCB Subcommittee on the Catechism and have been found to be in conformity with the *Catechism of the Catholic Church*, and so are deemed to be in accord with Catholic moral principles.

Organizational Structure

There are five units in each book corresponding to the five themes. There are two lessons in every unit. Each lesson is designed to be used in a 45-minute setting, with additional activities suggested to expand the lesson for longer class periods. Each lesson begins and ends with prayer. Suggestions are offered for those who wish to teach two lessons in one class period.

Each lesson flows through three steps: (1) Engage, which activates the child's knowledge of the lesson theme and helps relate the theme to experience; (2) Teach, where the concepts are taught and students begin to connect them to concrete situations; and (3) Apply, where students begin to integrate what they have learned into daily living and make a concrete faith choice.

Each lesson introduces students to a moral virtue related to family and community living, and helps them begin to practice the skills required to live that virtue and make it a personal habit.

Teaching Tips

RCL Benziger *Family Life* strives to teach children skills for living. Skills are learned by practice. Have students use role-play, games, and other interactive methods to practice these skills.

This series addresses many sensitive topics. Many children live in families with only one parent, split-time living between a divorced mother and father, and/or live with a stepparent or guardian. Help students understand that every family is different and that every family has problems. Help students to take pride in their families as they are, and not to feel ashamed that they are not perfect. Remind them from time to time that God loves all families.

Enjoy your time discussing the topics in RCL Benziger *Family Life* with your students. Let them know that the topics are serious, but do not suggest by word or deed that the topics are inappropriate or something to fear. Help the students to understand that all the themes that they are learning about are part of everyday living.

Child Safety Education

You do not need to be an expert in child safety to teach this course. You simply have to care about your students and want the best for them. RCL Benziger *Family Life* integrates child safety education into the regular flow of its lessons. Child safety skills are included in every lesson of every grade level. Your role here as a teacher is essential. Learning the skills for moral living and personal safety will last the children for a lifetime and help them to shape their lives.

Here are some suggestions to help you effectively present the materials:

▶ During this course of study students will learn to distinguish between appropriate and inappropriate touches. According to child safety experts, adults need not be afraid to touch children appropriately. For example, pats on the back and shoulder squeezes are okay. If a child wishes to hug you, accept the gesture, but maintain control of the hug (e.g. length, tightness) in a subtle way.

▶ While children are encouraged to express their feelings, they will sometimes reveal in public more than is appropriate. If you feel that the sharing gets too personal and is inappropriate, stop and thank the child for sharing. If you suspect that abuse may have occurred, speak to the child privately after class.

▶ Students will be taught what to do if they feel they have been touched inappropriately. If a child reports inappropriate touching to you, you have an obligation to report it. Every state and local community has its own established procedures to follow when reporting child abuse. Be familiar with those for your local area and follow them carefully. Also report the incident to the person in charge at your parish or school.

▶ As the teacher you must be prepared if a student reports inappropriate touching or another form of abuse. If a child reports they are being abused to you:

— Give thanks to God that the child feels safe enough with you to share this burden.

— Be prepared to let the child talk for as long as they need.

— Avoid asking questions; do not interview or interrogate; but do take notes, if possible, so that you can report accurately what the child says.

— Respect the child's privacy; do not discuss the situation with the child in public or anywhere that others may overhear. Consider what you have been told as privileged information that should only be shared with the proper authorities.

— Affirm the child's feelings; help them to see that they are doing the proper thing; let the child know that it is okay to feel frightened or afraid, sad and even relieved.

— Be honest about what will happen next ("I have to report what you told me to the police. They will want to talk with you. I will stay with you until . . .").

— Thank the child for speaking to you; let the child know how brave they are for speaking up.

Family Life Resources to Use with the Family

Each unit of RCL Benziger *Family Life* provides components to support the partnership between the teacher/catechist and the family.

Parent Connection

One of the most important resources is the Parent Connection magazine, which comes with each student text. The Parent Connection component informs the parents on what their child is learning, and instructs parents to help their child apply what has been learned. It also includes parenting tips for raising a Catholic family and suggestions of how to respond to children's questions concerning human sexuality. These grade level specific magazines are available only in English.

Hablando de la sexualidad con mis hijos is an informative and colorful 32-page booklet written for Spanish-reading parents. It offers background material on the five unit themes and assists parents in speaking about sexuality issues with their child of various ages. In addition, it addresses specific issues in Latino family life.

Student Edition

Core Lessons: The ten core lessons of each grade level student book explore, develop, and apply the moral teachings of the Catholic Church as they relate to the daily life of the Christian family. Parents may teach these lessons at home or enlist the help of their parish or school. Every lesson relies on parental involvement to be successful.

Family Time: Two Family Time pages open each unit of every student book. Written to the parents, these take-home pages inform the parents of the content to be studied in the coming lessons in the unit, focus on the spiritual and practical needs of the family, and offer suggestions on ways that the family can live a healthy and holy life.

Online Resources

Letters to the Family: Six customizable English and Spanish sample family letters are provided online. Sending letters home to parents is one way to keep them actively involved in their child's learning. There is a "Begin the Year" letter and one for each unit of every book.

Catholic Parenting 101: A wide variety of parent resources are also available online at RCLBFamilyLife.com offering articles and tips to help parents to fulfill their role as the primary educators of their children. These materials are updated frequently and cover a wide variety of topics such as parenting skills, spirituality in the home, keeping children safe, and speaking to children about difficult topics.

What Is a *Family Life* Catechist?

As a catechist or religion teacher you teach children about the Catholic faith and give witness to what you believe. You assist in the faith formation of the young people entrusted to your care. You join a long line of dedicated believers who have answered God's call to share their faith with others. Like these past catechists, you have been touched by your experience of Jesus Christ and are unable to keep the Good News to yourself.

In your role you assist parents in the faith formation of their children by making the teachings of the Catholic Church more explicit

and helping the children to celebrate their faith and to apply the Church's teachings to their lives.

Catechists echo the Word of God to help others deepen their understanding of the faith. You may be a little daunted by this responsibility and ministry. You might even wonder if it is more than you bargained for when you were asked and accepted the invitation to teach this *Family Life* course. Relax! Great saints, such as Moses, Jeremiah, Peter and Mary had similar concerns; but with God's help, they did great things—and you will too!

Qualities of a Catechist

The *National Directory for Catechesis* (NDC) published by the U.S. bishops in 2005 names key qualities of effective catechists and Catholic school religion teachers—qualities that you already possess. Catechists and religion teachers:

- ▶ ***Respond to a vocational call from the Lord*** to bring others to faith in him. As you catechize others you also continue to grow in your own faith and in your own knowledge of the faith.

- ▶ ***Give witness to the Gospel message of Jesus Christ*** as taught by his Church. You believe in this message and in her power to change the lives of all who believe in it. You model for others what it means to follow Jesus.

- ▶ ***Make a commitment to the Church*** to express the teachings of the Catholic Church as clearly and accurately as you can. You grow in understanding of the Catholic faith as you teach the Church's wisdom.

- ▶ ***Build a faith community among your learners*** because you have experienced its importance in your own life, through parish life and through your love of and participation in the Eucharist. You encourage and prepare your students to live virtuous lives of forgiveness, reconciliation and peacemaking.

- ▶ **Implement the mission of the Church** to proclaim the Gospel to the world by responding to the needs of others and by teaching your students to do the same.

- ▶ **Develop the skills and abilities needed** to conduct effective catechetical sessions, present complex concepts so that they are clearly understood, and care for your students appropriately.

You can read more about the catechetical ministry in chapters 2 and 8 of the *National Directory for Catechesis*.

Qualities of a *Family Life* Catechist

In addition to the qualities of catechists and religion teachers named in the NDC, the *Family Life* catechist will also show in particular a:

- ▶ **Dialogic Partnership with Families.** The RCL Benziger *Family Life* series recognizes and celebrates the parents' primary role and responsibility in guiding their children's formation in all topics, not just those related to family life education. The *Family Life* catechist is to respect the parents' role and be willing to assist them in fulfilling this role in whatever ways they can. The *Family Life* catechist uses all means possible to keep parents informed about what the children are learning and to assist parents in helping their children integrate what they have learned into the family's life. Catechists will encourage parent participation and communication,

and will listen attentively when parents speak. As much as possible, they will try to implement the parents' wishes for their children.

- ▶ **Sensitivity to Diverse Family Settings.** Children live in many diverse settings. Some live with their biological mothers and fathers; some are adopted. Some children live in families affected by divorce; others in families affected by sickness or death. Some have many siblings; others have none. The *Family Life* catechist will know their students well and will be sensitive to their home situations. When the program emphasizes the Church's teaching on the Christian family, the *Family Life* catechist will help the students to understand the blessings found in all families.

- ▶ **Comfort with Human Sexuality.** Although the program is designed so that parents may teach issues of human reproduction in the home, the RCL Benziger *Family Life* series, in every grade level, still presents the Church's teachings on human sexuality in age-appropriate ways. The *Family Life* catechist needs to be able to speak about these topics with dignity and grace. The catechist must believe that the human body is a sacred gift from God, and is something to be treated with respect and admiration, and not with fear or guilt. The catechist needs to be able to talk with their students without feeling awkwardness or shame, and must welcome the curious questions of children openly and responsibly. Teaching tips throughout the series will help you to do so in appropriate ways respecting prudence and modesty.

What Will I Teach?

Each grade level is organized around the same five themes. Each of these unit themes are presented according to the student's developmental readiness and level of comprehension. Each unit extends into the home through a variety of special parent materials.

Theme 1—God's Gift of Family

[T]he family has the mission to guard, reveal and communicate love, and this is a living reflection of and a real sharing in God's love for humanity and the love of Christ the Lord for the Church His bride.

FAMILIARIS CONSORTIO 17

Family living is the initial theme of the program, setting the context to explore all the themes. In every grade, students will develop the skills and knowledge they need to live a healthy and holy life within their family, for now and in the future. Students will develop these key Catholic values in association with this theme:

▶ An appreciation that the family is the person's first community

▶ An understanding that beliefs and values are developed, shared and lived within the family

▶ An awareness that healthy families provide social and spiritual meaning for all members

▶ A recognition that each family member is responsible for the life of the Catholic family

Theme 2—God's Gift of Self

Ideally, each person strives to be physically developed, psychologically integrated, interpersonally responsible, and spiritually holy. [In addition, there is] the wider, more universal calling to be loving and chaste, whatever one's vocation is in life.

HUMAN SEXUALITY PAGE 26

In this unit, students will be challenged to understand the physical, emotional and spiritual development of themselves and others. They will also learn to examine their motives honestly, and appreciate their strengths and weaknesses. Through these efforts, they will grow in realistic self-esteem, a valuable component of a person's emotional health and a valuable tool to overcome negative peer pressure and temptations within the culture. Students will develop these key Catholic values in association with this theme:

▶ An understanding of how to express their emotions appropriately

▶ A responsible attitude toward one's physical health and care of the body

▶ A sense of self as a gift necessary to form healthy relationships

▶ An awareness that spiritual growth is a life-long process, just like physical and emotional development

▶ The formation of their conscience, shaped by authentic Church teaching, that will help them to make good moral choices

Theme 3—God's Gift of Life

At this tense moment in our history, when external wars and internal violence make us so conscious of death, an affirmation of the sanctity of human life by renewed attention to the family is imperative. HUMAN LIFE IN OUR DAY 83

In this unit, students will grow in their appreciation of the sacredness of human life and of their own potential to love and serve selflessly.

Students will develop these key Catholic values in association with this theme:

- A reverence for human life, and all that supports and contributes to it
- An understanding of the inherent dignity of the human person as created in God's image and likeness, regardless of productivity, role, function, or social status
- A recognition that every stage of human life, from conception until natural death, is precious
- An awareness of the challenges that exist to the sanctity of life and the moral strength required from every person in order to respond to these challenges

Theme 4—God's Gift of Love

Like all our human powers and freedoms, sexuality, a gift from God, can be channeled for good or ill. Each of us is entrusted by God with the responsibility to guide and direct this gift wisely and lovingly. HUMAN SEXUALITY PAGE 10

In this unit, students will develop gradually a wholesome understanding of sexuality and its place in Catholic family life. They will learn, as appropriate by their age, that human sexuality is intimately connected with the gifts of love and life, with strength and service, with compassion and discipline. Through lessons on healthy habits and moral virtues, they will learn the need to live healthy and holy lives. Students will develop these key Catholic values in association with this theme:

- An appreciation of the critical role gender has in the life of every person
- An understanding of the importance of the virtue of chastity and healthy attitudes about sexuality for living a moral life

- A respect for the reproductive abilities of the human body and its connection to full personhood and family life

Theme 5—God's Gift of Community

The truth of globalization as a process and its fundamental ethical criterion are given by the unity of the human family and its development towards what is good. Hence a sustained commitment is needed so as to promote a person-based and community-oriented cultural process of world-wide integration that is open to transcendence.
CARITAS IN VERITATE 42

The family, as the domestic Church, is one of the key communities in which people live as disciples of Jesus and where discipleship is taught. An understanding of how people live with and relate to one another is an essential component of discipleship and family living. In this unit, students will learn the virtues and skills needed for a just society. These lessons will prepare them to take their responsible places in society both now and in the future. Students will learn how to answer the call to Christian social ministry. Students will develop these key Catholic values in association with this theme:

- A respect for interpersonal relationships and human interaction
- An appreciation for the cooperation and mutual benefit needed for a healthy society
- A willingness to implement Catholic social teaching such as solidarity and stewardship
- A recognition for all Christians to work together for the coming of God's reign of justice, mercy and peace

How Will I Teach?

Under the guidance of the Holy Spirit, catechists powerfully influence those being catechized by their faithful proclamation of the Gospel of Jesus Christ and the transparent example of their Christian lives.

NATIONAL DIRECTORY FOR CATECHESIS 29E

The catechetical ministry has been nurtured and renewed in recent years by the publication of three documents: The *Catechism of the Catholic Church* (1993), the *General Directory for Catechesis* (1997), and the *National Directory for Catechesis* (2005).

The Catechism (CCC) provides a systematic presentation of the contents of the Catholic faith. The General Directory (GDC) defines the goals, principles and guidelines of catechesis. The National Directory (NDC) applies these principles of catechesis to catechetical ministry in the United States. The RCL Benziger *Family Life* series reflects these key documents throughout.

Divine Methodology

The National Directory, in chapter 4, examines the use of methodology in catechesis. Beginning with the divine methodology (God's self-Revelation to us through Jesus and the Holy Spirit), the NDC reminds us that God has revealed everything we know and believe about our faith. Catechists are encouraged to follow this methodology by engaging "persons and communities in light of their circumstances and their capacity to accept and interpret Revelation" (*NDC 28*).

Human Methodologies

The second part of chapter 4 of the National Directory focuses on the elements of human methodology. It emphasizes that, because learning takes place in different ways, we should rely on a variety of methods to pass on our faith to students, just as God has done. The NDC offers eight different human methodologies that catechists can use (*see NDC, 29 A-H*). All eight are featured throughout the RCL Benziger *Family Life* series.

1. *Learning through Human Experience:* We respond to God's invitation through our human experiences. Each RCL Benziger *Family Life* lesson begins by engaging the child's interest and imagination and helping them relate the lesson concept to their own experiences.

2. *Learning by Discipleship:* We learn the Way of Jesus Christ by choosing to follow him and do what he asks us. In each lesson students are introduced to Jesus' teaching and learn how to live and act as Jesus' disciples.

3. *Learning within the Christian Community:* The witness of the Church shows children how to believe, worship and take up the Gospel call to service. In each lesson, students are taught the skills that will help them to live as responsible members of the Catholic Church.

4. **Learning within the Christian Family:** The Christian family is usually the first experience children have of living within community. The family offers the first and best environment for growth in faith. RCL Benziger *Family Life* fosters a partnership between home, school and parish. Students learn family living skills, and resources are provided to help families grow in faith, hope, and love together.

5. **Learning through the Witness of the Catechist:** You have a powerful influence on your students' faith formation. You influence them by the knowledge you share, by your attitudes and actions, and by the witness you give that your faith is important to you. You model for them what is important and what is not. You show them what it means to live a Christian life. RCL Benziger *Family Life* provides you with sure guidance on being a positive witness.

6. **Learning by Heart:** When we "learn by heart," we make knowledge or a skill our own. We have it in memory for life. Students develop a strong Catholic identity and literacy by learning key definitions, moral teachings, and Catholic practices and prayers. The Catholics Believe and Catholic Family Album features in RCL Benziger *Family Life* provide the students treasures of the Church that strengthen their Catholic identity.

7. **Making a Commitment to Live the Christian Life:** Faith statements remain merely words until students make a commitment to live them out in their own lives. In every lesson the RCL Benziger *Family Life* series invites students to make a concrete choice and commitment to act upon what they have learned.

8. **Learning by Apprenticeship:** Children are quick studies: they watch what adults and older children do, and then they imitate what they have seen. This imitation is at the heart of learning by apprenticeship. Students are encouraged to find adults whom they can trust and learn from. Learning approaches used within each lesson encourage students to learn from others and to practice imitating moral, healthy and holy behavior.

Know Your Seventh Graders

Whether you are a seasoned professional teacher or a first-year catechist, it's always good to stop now and then, place yourself in the shoes of your students, and imagine who they are. What are their abilities? How do they view themselves, you, their families, and the world? The thumbnail sketch on this page offers some general characteristics of twelve-year-olds drawn from current research. Only you and the child's parents, after careful observation and dialogue with your students, can know the extent to which each of your students corresponds to this norm. So get to know your students well.

Physical and Emotional Characteristics

- They are in their early adolescent years and experiencing the transition period between childhood and adulthood.

- This is a time of great development (physical, moral, emotional, social, psychological, and spiritual).

- Many are beginning to show interest in members of the other sex.

- Seventh graders value peer acceptance and find it important to belong. Conformity can bring feelings of safety and comfort.

Learning Skills

- Twelve-years-olds are capable of some abstract thought.

- They are developing a sense of identity. A stress on creativity in all its forms when creating assignments can help mold a strong sense of self-worth.

- They are able to participate in planning and participating in long-range assignments. This will help the seventh grader to develop a sense of accountability and responsibility.

- Seventh graders enjoy opportunities to talk and think through issues as a class.

Religious Growth

- Because they enjoy being part of a group, seventh graders are more likely to grow in their faith within their peer community of believers.

- Some students will wonder if the Church has any meaning for them and question where religion fits into their lives.

- Adolescence is a time where thoughts are turned inward again. Twelve-years-olds are concerned about themselves. It is helpful for students to know that Jesus suffered growing pains too.

- The student's focus is on their peers. They enjoy working in groups to plan for and celebrate the Sacraments and prayer services.

Conclusion

All of these qualities and abilities affect the child's role in the family as well. They are no longer children and yet, do not have the responsibilities and privileges of adults. This may cause strain on the parent-child relationship as seventh graders yearn for more freedom from parents who are not yet ready to loosen the reins. As they begin to take the responsibility that comes with freedom, you can help them develop good decisions making skills by helping them to critically reflect on moral decisions they will be facing. These critical reflection skills can help students become more responsible members of their families and society.

Partnering with the Family

The classroom has become the setting for most curricula, and too many family materials are designed to support the classroom teaching. Gradually the family's central role of overseeing the moral development of their children has been eroded. RCL Benziger *Family Life* changes that equation and puts the parents back in their primary and essential role. The *Family Life* materials help to foster a partnership between the family and the parish that is needed for successful faith formation.

The Home

Parents are the first and most influential shapers of their children's moral values and character. The Catholic Church has consistently called for parents to reclaim this role and has offered them assistance in doing so. "The Church holds that it is her duty to give parents back confidence in their own capabilities and help them to carry out their task" (*The Truth and Meaning of Human Sexuality* 47). RCL Benziger *Family Life* places the home and the parents at the center of the program. Parents can use the RCL Benziger *Family Life* materials with confidence knowing that they conform to and implement appropriate

Church documents, and that they have been found to be in conformity with the *Catechism of the Catholic Church*.

The School and Parish

Several Church documents call for parishes and schools to support parents in their role as moral educators. RCL Benziger *Family Life* provides the essential resources needed to provide a substantial and effective moral catechesis for all children.

The Child

The child is at the heart of all family life education. RCL Benziger *Family Life* introduces children to the Catholic Church's moral teachings as they apply to family living, helps them to understand these teachings appropriately by age, and teaches practical ways to follow these teachings in making moral decisions.

The *Family Life* program assures children of their worth and dignity, and helps them take pride in their families, regardless of its problems. Children are affirmed in their human dignity at each stage of development. They are taught to make good moral decisions by applying sound moral principles and skills. They are challenged to deepen their moral perspective and to take on greater responsibility each year. Most importantly, children develop the habits (living the virtues) and build the skills they need to live healthy and holy moral lives. RCL Benziger *Family Life* provides young people with the foundation they will need in the future as they respond to God's call to love their way through life.

Child Safety Education

This edition of the RCL Benziger *Family Life* has been revised to assist parishes and dioceses in their effort to implement the 2002 *Charter for the Protection of Children*. The *Family Life* series supports safe environment training to the Church's children and youth, and to provide support to parents and teachers who are responsible for the education and safety of the children. This revision puts into practice this advice from the National Center for Missing and Exploited Children (NCMEC):

> Programs on child safety . . . should be designed to increase children's ability to recognize and avoid potentially dangerous situations and help better protect themselves. Equally important is the development of self-esteem at every level of the educational process, because children with self-confidence are less likely to be victimized. (*Guidelines for Programs to Reduce Child Victimization* page 4.)

RCL Benziger *Family Life* integrates child safety education into a holistic approach to family life education. In every lesson of every grade level, children are provided with opportunities to develop the knowledge, self-confidence, and assertiveness skills that they will need to recognize dangerous situations, avoid them if possible, and respond appropriately in time of need.

RCL Benziger *Family Life* is also designed to help reduce guilt feelings among children, encourage them to speak frequently and freely with their parents and other trusted adults, express their feelings appropriately, and to practice forgiving themselves and others. All of these items reflect the best of safe environment educational theory.

The Importance of Repetition and Reinforcement

According to research commissioned by the NCMEC, the most successful child safety programs were those that were offered over a significant period of time and provided children multiple opportunities to learn, interact with and apply the rules of child safety. These programs taught children how to recognize, avoid and protect themselves from dangerous situations, modeled for the children appropriate behavior, had the children actively rehearse that behavior, and provided consistent feedback and reinforcement.

Children are given multiple opportunities over the ten lessons within each grade level to learn, interact with and apply the rules of child safety in an interactive manner as recommended by NCMEC. RCL Benziger *Family Life* meets the criteria and addresses the skills identified as important by the NCMEC. According to NCMEC, such education should teach children:

▶ Basic safety rules in an age appropriate manner.

▶ The difference between appropriate and inappropriate touching.

▶ To say "No" to any touch or action that causes them to feel unwelcome, uncomfortable, or confused.

How to respond to situations that cause them fear or discomfort.

The importance of open and honest communication with parents or guardians, and of identifying people they can trust in time when they need to talk to someone besides their parents

The child safety component of RCL Benziger *Family Life* has been carefully integrated into the series so that child safety issues and skills are seen as a normal part of the family life curriculum. Because parents have the primary responsibility for their children's safety, this series is designed to work in partnership with them.

Materials are designed so that parents can teach these important topics in the home or practice them once they have been taught in the school or religious education program. While the responsibility for protecting children from harm falls primarily on adults, children have the right to safety training and parishes have the obligation to provide such training. Protecting children helps to define us as a Church: Catholics protect children, provide them with a safe environment, and teach children what they can do to protect themselves.

You, as teacher or catechist, also have an essential role in supporting the parents. While you may not feel adequately prepared for your role, do not let that discourage you from moving ahead. Remember, you are teaching children the skills they need to protect themselves from harm.

Child Safety

Here are some basic rules to remember when teaching children safety issues:

- Avoid frightening the child.
- Use stories and examples to communicate the message, rather than lecturing.
- Show children how to respond to various situations and then practice what you show them.
- Listen carefully to what children say; teach them that adults will listen to and believe them.
- Help children feel good about themselves.
- Help them to understand that they are not responsible for the actions of adults or others.
- Avoid anything that might make children feel guilty because of the actions of others.

Catechetical Formation in Chaste Living

In November 2007 the United States Conference of Catholic Bishops approved the document *Catechetical Formation in Chaste Living: Guidelines for Curriculum Design and Publication.* Accordingly, the RCL Benziger *Family Life* series has been developed in conformity with the requirements of this document.

Created by the USCCB Committee on Catechesis (now the Committee on Evangelization and Catechesis), the Chaste Living guidelines were built upon the foundation laid by recent Church documents, namely, *Catechism of the Catholic Church, General Directory for Catechesis, National Directory for Catechesis,* and *United States Catholic Catechism for Adults.* These Chaste Living guidelines were also formed through a series of national consultations on the document. Through this consultation process, all the bishops of the United States and members of their catechetical and pastoral

ministry staffs offered corrections and changes to the document. Theologians, catechists, and experts in chaste living education also participated in this process by which the final document was produced.

The introduction to the guidelines ends with these words:

> [T]he Church continues to proclaim salvation in Christ Jesus and to invite men and women to follow his way. Though humanity is still wounded by sin, the Church continues to call all to trust in God's mercy, to turn away from sin, and to embrace the Good News. She continues to teach everyone how to live as Jesus did, instructing them in the message of the Ten Commandments, the Beatitudes, and the entire Gospel. She urges frequent reception of the sacraments, especially Penance and Reconciliation and the Eucharist, and cultivation of the virtues that enable people to lead a chaste and holy life (pg. 2).

The Chaste Living guidelines state that education for chaste living is essential to the formation of children and adolescents in the Catholic faith and "should be mandatory in Catholic schools and in parish religious education and youth ministry programs. This may be done in the form of a curriculum, a presentation for youth and/ or parents, or the use of other educational materials" (pg. 1).

This too is the vision and purpose of the RCL Benziger *Family Life* series: (1) to proclaim the salvation of Jesus and invite people to a life as his disciples; (2) to call people to trust in God's mercy, turn away from sin, and embrace the Good News; (3) to instruct people in the Church's moral teachings; (4) to encourage active participation in the Church's sacramental and worship life; and (5) to help people to cultivate the virtues so that they may live chaste and holy lives.

To help parishes, school, and programs of youth ministry accomplish this mandate, this series provides a variety of options for presenting the material, including classroom sessions, teaching at home, and large group intergenerational gatherings.

Here are some of the ways the RCL Benziger *Family Life* series implements the directives in the U.S. Bishops' document:

▸ The series was developed following the *Catechism of the Catholic Church*, the *General Directory for Catechesis*, and the *National Directory for Catechesis*.

▸ Catechesis on Catholic faith and morals and on the virtues is presented as an essential part of every lesson.

▸ All catechesis on chaste living takes place within the faith community.

▸ Catechists and teachers are seen as assisting parents in the formation of their children.

▸ Catechists and teachers are provided with a clear knowledge of Catholic teaching.

▸ Parents are provided with the resources they need to fulfill their particular responsibility to catechize their children in faith and morals. Tips are provided throughout the take-home and online resources and the Parent Connection booklets to help prepare parents to speak to the issues addressed throughout the series.

▸ Parents are recognized as having the primary role of providing specific education in human sexuality. Human Reproduction Booklet A and Human Reproduction Booklet B are provided for two levels so that parents can explain human sexuality at home. These booklets are generally used during the fifth and sixth grade, when the children are entering puberty; but these two booklets can be used at older grades levels as well. Proper references are made to human anatomy or physiology, but only to the degree necessary to teach morality and virtuous living.

Learning Outcomes for Chaste Living

In writing this document, the U.S. Bishops desired that each baptized person:

▸ cherish human dignity as made in the image and likeness of God.

▸ faithfully reflect that image in a life conformed to new life in Christ.

▸ deepen the relationship with Christ and the Church through frequent prayer and celebration of the Sacraments, especially the Sacrament of Penance and Reconciliation and the Sacrament of the Eucharist.

▸ embrace joyfully the call to love and live chastely either as a married person or as a celibate person.

Each of these desired outcomes is promoted within every level of the RCL Benziger *Family Life* series.

Models for Implementation of RCL Benziger *Family Life*

In Catholic Schools

Most Catholic schools offer the *Family Life* series in ten teaching blocks, corresponding with the ten lessons in each grade level. Any one of the following three models can help you implement the program into your existing curriculum. Detailed instructions for using each of these is provided in the Program Director's Manual.

Two-Week Course

Set aside two weeks during the year and teach one lesson per day during the regularly scheduled religion class. The lesson plans provided in the Teacher Edition are designed to be taught in a 45-minute class period. There are also plenty of suggestions for how to expand the lesson for longer class sessions. This approach provides a special emphasis on family life curriculum and enables you to actively engage parents during this time.

Ten-Week Course

Teach this series during your regular religion class one day a week over a period of ten weeks. Pick a day during the week so that students will become accustomed to having the lessons on the same day. For example, if you pick Thursday, the students will know they will have a *Family Life* lesson on Thursdays. Parents will also come to expect this consistency and will learn to set aside time before, during and after the lesson is taught in order to reinforce what has been learned.

Ten-Month Course

This approach allows you to reinforce family life curriculum throughout the entire school year. Designate one day a month as Family Life Day. A lesson from the *Family Life* series would be taught during the scheduled religion class, and all other classes would emphasize the importance of engaging the family. On this day, celebrate the family in a variety of ways.

Use the *Family Life* series as an opportunity to engage families more actively in the life of your school and in the life of their children.

In the Parish

Finding time within the catechetical year calendar can be challenging. However, because of the its flexibility, the *Family Life* series can be used without taking away from the time needed for regular religious instruction. Detailed instructions for using each of these models is provided in the Program Director's Manual.

Supplement to Religion Period

Add thirty minutes to a regular religion period ten times a year. This approach will enable you to flow from the regular lesson into the *Family Life* lesson. A correlation chart is available online at www.RCLBFamilyLife.com showing how *Family Life* can be integrated into your religion curriculum.

Condense into Five Sessions

Each grade level of *Family Life* is organized into five units. This makes it possible to condense the teaching of the ten lessons into five sessions. Lesson plans are provided in the Program Director's Manual detailing how this can best be accomplished.

Summer Program

Promote and strengthen family life during your summer programming. Include one hour each day for *Family Life*. Encourage family members to actively participate in their children's studies.

Intergenerational Sessions

Bring families together for five evenings during the year for a Family Life Night. Schedule a two-hour session for family activities and lessons taken from *Family Life*. Lesson plans are provided in the Program Director's Manual for teaching a unit in one lesson.

Scope and Sequence for Grade 7

	God's Gift of Family	God's Gift of Self	God's Gift of Life	God's Gift of Love	God's Gift of Community
Faith Concepts	The Holy Spirit helps us to forgive; Using the gift of free will to say yes to God	Spiritual maturity means becoming like Jesus; Complementariness in genders	The human body is a temple of the Holy Spirit; Honoring the dignity of the person	Our loving relationships are to reflect the loving communion of the Trinity; Chastity is integrating our sexuality into life and love	God created us to share love; God created us to live in community
Virtues	Compassion; Responsibility	Resilience; Diligence	Wellness; Temperance; Prudence	Charity; Chastity	Conscientiousness; Solidarity
Family Skills	Conflict resolution; Dealing with peer pressure	Self-assessment of my attributes and attitudes	Keeping a health checklist; Making a prayer pledge	Developing an action plan; Responding to pressure	Discerning messages in the media; Developing and growing friendships
Catholic Family Album	Sts. Michael, Gabriel and Raphael; St. Hilary of Poitiers	St. Gertrude the Great; St. Paul of Tarsus	Catholic Hospitals; Catholic Charities	Pope Benedict XVI, St. Josemaria Escriva	The Samaritan Woman; Communion of Saints
Catechism of the Catholic Church	CCC 2843	CCC 1308, 2333	CCC 2288–2294, 2519	CCC 221, 1022–1024, 1337, 1604, 2338, 2345	CCC 1829, 1972, 2342–2343

God's Gift of Family

Background

"The relationships between the members of the family community are inspired and guided by the law of 'free giving.' By respecting and fostering personal dignity in each and every one as the only basis for value, this free giving takes the form of heartfelt acceptance, encounter and dialogue, disinterested availability, generous service and deep solidarity" (Familiaris Consortio 43).

THE FAMILY IS THE PRIMARY COMMUNITY OF LIFE and love. This is especially true for children just about to enter adolescence. Soon most young people of this age will be adding friends or a peer group into their lives, which will play a very important role. Usually, these connections are a mixed blessing. Sometimes friends will exert a positive influence, or pressure, on young people. At other times, they will not. It is important to underscore for children the importance of the family connection during this period of their life. The influence of family relations offers a full range of possible outcomes.

This movement toward a community of their peers and away from family is a necessary step toward maturity. As they take this step, young adolescents often experience difficulty in relating to their parents and older members of their family. There is often miscommunication and a lack of understanding among family members. Working on respectful communication and action can help children and their parents surmount these difficulties. This requires time, patience and skill.

Additional Background

Catechism of the Catholic Church: §§ 1657, 1882, 2201–2203, 2205, 2225–2226, 2685

POSITIVE AND LIFE-ENHANCING FAMILY RELATIONS are characterized by certain qualities. In the passage above, Pope John Paul II identifies several of these qualities. First, there is "heartfelt acceptance." This quality of relating forms the bedrock of family life. Being accepted is among the deepest of human needs. We want to be with others and the entrance to belonging is acceptance. Each of us seeks to be included with all our uniqueness and idiosyncrasies. Being accepted by others in this way, especially by those closest to us, creates the climate where we can accept ourselves and others. The goodness of our very being is affirmed and valued through being accepted.

Second, the pope names "disinterested availability" as another quality of positive and life-enhancing relationships. This quality identifies the need for others to be available to us for meeting our needs. Many point to a positive value of cell phones because they can connect us with others. They allow for greater availability between family members and friends. Third, in the family there is the possibility of "generous service." Generous service goes in all directions, namely, parents serve their children and children do the same for parents.

Sometimes it is helpful to reflect on the most important things in our lives. Consider a reflection focused on being aware of what our family experiences offer each of us. Reflect on the specific influences the family has on our thoughts, our personal values and on our sense of what's really worthwhile in life. Parents can tell their children how they have made their lives better. We all can benefit from a greater awareness of how our family experience influences who we are today.

For Reflection

Read and reflect on the following:

"Family communion can only be preserved and perfected through a great spirit of sacrifice. It requires, in fact, a ready and generous openness of each and all to understanding, to forbearance, to pardon, to reconciliation" (Familiaris Consortio *21).*

▶ How well do I openly communicate with my family? How disinterested is my availability? How generous is my service?

▶ What might I do to create an environment of awareness, availability and service in my class community?

Child Safety

Approximately 800,000 children are abused in the United States each year. Teenage girls are the ones most likely to be sexually abused. The lessons in this unit provide an opportunity to teach skills to keep students safe. Lesson 1 addresses the children's right to say no to any touch or sign of affection that they feel inappropriate or are uncomfortable with. Lesson 2 explains that if they feel pressured by anyone to engage in physical contact that they think is inappropriate or to watch or hear something that is sexually explicit, they should get away from the situation as quickly as they can and then tell a trusted adult about what happened.

Family Time

Partnering with the Family

Religious formation of children is the primary responsibility of parents or guardians. The Family Time pages that begin each unit of *Family Life* help parents and other members of the family fulfill this responsibility. By sending these materials home, you are working in partnership with the parents to help them and their children to continue to grow as a healthy and holy family.

LESSON 1 PLANNER

Goal: To examine good communication skills within family relationships and how birth order and changes during puberty can affect the way we interact

Engage
Page 33

Objective
To explore the meaning of family relationships

Family Time
Ensure that each student tears out their Family Time page to complete at home.

Pray
Give thanks to God for each member of the family.

Focus
Share meaning and origin of family names.

Discover
Discuss the influence of birth order within family relationships.

Teach
Page 34

Objective
To connect compassion to communication

Focus
Growing in Virtue: Compassion

Explore
Read, discuss and summarize the importance of listening and communicating with compassion.
Catholics Believe: Compassion is an unconditional love.

Connect
Pick a scenario and show what compassion looks like.

Apply
Page 36

Objective
To practice the skill of listening in conflict situations

Focus
Discuss opinions about a popular book, movie or celebrity.

Discover
Catholic Family Album: The three archangels

Integrate
Role-play using the skills of good communication.

Pray
Pray for angelic assistance in communicating with compassion.

Vocabulary Preview

Birth Order—describes the sequence of offspring and thus particular position within the family according to when born

Blended Family—a family created when adults with children from an earlier marriage enter a new marriage

Compassion—the character strength of being able to identify with the situation and feelings of another; built on an attitude of equality

Generation—a group of related people born around the same time

Mercy—loving kindness in the context of forgiveness and compassion

Materials Needed

▶ writing paper
▶ pens, pencils
▶ art supplies
▶ slips of paper
▶ Bible
▶ Lesson 1 Activity Masters

Call to Prayer

God, you have placed each of us in a family in this time and place. Bless each family and strengthen their bonds of love and loyalty. May your Spirit of peace settle in our hearts and guide our habits. Amen.

Family Relationships

Family History

When you were quite young, your world revolved around a special someone known to you as "me." As you grew older, your world expanded to include "my family." When you grew older yet, you saw that your family came from generations of families. A generation is a group of related people born and living around the same time. Even if their names are long forgotten, you have hundreds of relatives in past generations.

In some families, a child grows up with both birth parents. But, for different reasons, this does not always happen. There are children who grow up in single-parent families, and there are other children who do not live with either birth parent.

Some children are adopted by new families. Other children grow up in blended families. This type of family is created when adults with children from an earlier marriage enter a new marriage. The members of both families "blend" into a new family.

Within a family, a child has a particular position, or birth order. This is the order according to when you were born. There can be advantages and disadvantages to your birth order. The oldest child, or first born, may face more expectations or receive more responsibility. The youngest child may be tired of being the "baby sister" or "baby brother." The middle child may feel overlooked.

As you grow older, the way you relate to your family will change. Some of the people in your life will have certain expectations of you. These expectations might be based on your family birth order. So be aware of the advantages of your place in your family, too. Try to see all the possibilities it can bring.

> This lesson will help you to:
> - **explore** the meaning of family relationships.
> - **connect** compassion to communication.
> - **practice** the skill of listening in conflict situations.

 How does your birth order or being an only child affect you?

Family Relationships 11

Teaching Tip

Child Safety: You will find child safety teaching suggestions embedded within each of the lessons of this course. Safe environment training gives children the helpful skills to play their part in protecting themselves from would-be offenders. The key skills, put into play in various ways appropriate to the children's ages, are those that help the child RECOGNIZE inappropriate behavior, RESPOND to it effectively, and REPORT the situation to a trusted adult. Teach the children to recognize when they feel unsafe or uncomfortable using examples from their lives. Practice saying "no." Help them list who are trusted adults in their lives.

Objective

To explore the meaning of family relationships

Pray

Open the lesson with a prayer giving thanks to God for each member of our families.

Focus

Have students take turns saying aloud their full name. Then ask them to share any information about their name, its meaning, origin, family connection, etc.

Discover

- ▶ Read "Family History." Allow students to ask questions about the reading.

- ▶ Group students according to their birth order: only child, first born, second, etc. Have each group create a list of blessings and burdens of their birth order.

- ▶ Discuss each group's list, focusing on the influence of parental expectations.

- ▶ Inquire: According to your birth order, what do you contribute to your family?

- ▶ Time permitting, have each student create a symbol that communicates what their family is all about. For example, if the family is exceptionally courageous, then use a lion in the drawing of a symbol.

Objective

To practice the skill of listening in conflict situations

Focus

Discuss a topic familiar to the students, for example, a book, movie or celebrity. Invite students to discuss their opinions about the topic. Observe how they discuss it to see if they listen and talk with compassion.

Discover

Read the Catholic Family Album box. Inquire with students on how during their Focus discussion they protected the truth, spoke honestly and listened.

Integrate

▶ Read "Resolving Conflicts." Review the Do's and Do Not's List.

▶ Pair-up students to have them complete the activity on the page.

▶ Time permitting, have volunteers present one of their scenarios to the class.

Pray

Invite students to pray for assistance from their guardian angel in speaking the truth in love and communicating with compassion.

Catholic Family Album

Angels are God's chief messengers. The word "angel" comes from a Greek word meaning "messenger." Michael, Gabriel and Raphael are **the three archangels** named in Scripture and have been named patrons of good communication. Each archangel points to essential elements in good communication. Michael protects the truth, so we ought to speak honestly. Gabriel announces the will of God, so we need to listen to who is speaking. Raphael guides one to happiness, so we should follow good principles that lead us to God, the true source of our happiness.

Resolving Conflicts

Good communication does not eliminate conflict in family life. Good communication, however, can help resolve conflict. There are good communication principles that you can use when you find yourself in a conflict situation. Some of those principles are listed in the chart below.

Pair up with a partner and role-play the principles on the list. One person could role-play a "Do's" principle and the other a "Do Not's" principle. Accent the positive and negative consequences of each principle by exaggerating your communication. Identify a real-life situation and ask each other, which would you rather have happen to you: the "Do's" or the "Do Not's."

Then choose one of the Do's principles and tell how you will use it.

DO's	DO NOT's
__Calm down and cool off	__Yell or use the silent treatment
__Say exactly how you feel	__Use labels or put-downs
__Keep eye contact	__Interrupt while the other person is talking
__Stick to the issue, not to personalities	__Think only of how the conflict affects you
__Listen, without interrupting, to the other person's point of view	__Insist that the other person is the only one at fault
__Talk about the part you may have played in causing the conflict	__Refer to conflicts from the past
__Decide together on an acceptable solution	__Insist on getting your own way

Do's Principle: _____

I will _____

_____

_____

_____

14   Family Relationships

Extending the Lesson

Using Activity Master 1B: Use the Activity Master "Seeing All Sides." This activity engages the students in thinking about all perspectives involved in a situation. You can use this activity as a discussion starter or in conjunction with the Teach section of this lesson.

Animals with Attitude: Have students make cartoons depicting animals avoiding or mishandling conflict situations. Animals with attitude might include porcupine (bristles to protect or show anger), hippo (washes or whines), dog (always there for you or annoys you), weasel (blames everyone or skillful in getting things done), elephant (never forgets the good or bad), zebra (runs away from conflict) ostrich (avoids conflict).

Activity Master 1A

Name

Picture Your Family

Totem poles use symbols from nature to tell about a family or tribe. Animals are often included to show special qualities such as wisdom, strength, swiftness, and so on. Answer each question. Then draw a symbol on each part of the totem pole.

What quality do you most admire in your family?

_____

What quality do you most admire in yourself?

_____

What quality has your family passed on to you?

_____

What do you contribute to your family?

_____

What would you like to pass on to the next generation?

_____

© RCL Publishing LLC

Family Life Grade 7

Activity Master 1B

Name

Seeing All Sides

Read "It's like this:" and fill in "I'm thinking . . ." and "My parents are thinking . . ." Cut out the rectangle, fold on the dotted lines, and glue as shown. Look at one side at a time. Are there some reasonable ideas on each side? How can the differences be resolved?

My parents are thinking . . .	It's like this:	I'm thinking . . .
	I met some neat kids at the mall. They're a lot of fun, and they don't do anything bad like shoplift or anything. They want me to meet them at the mall again next Saturday.	
	My grandparents and aunts and uncles got together and sent me a pretty big check for a birthday present. I'm not sure how to spend it. I want to go shopping by myself.	
	Both Mom and Dad work during the week, so they have a lot of errands and stuff to do on Saturday. By the time I help, I don't have much time to do things with my friends.	
	My little brother wants to do everything I do. He's OK, but I don't want him hanging around with me and my friends all the time.	

Glue

© RCL Publishing LLC

Family Life Grade 7

How to Find It
How to Use It

Step 1: Click & Select

Go to RCLBFamilyLife.com
Click on the link for activities.
Then select the activity master you need.

Step 2: Print & Copy

Print each activity master in advance.
Then copy enough for everyone in the class.

Step 3: Share & Discuss

Once students have completed the activity,
have them share and discuss their responses.

Goal: To explore family values and understand how they influence our decisions to live virtuously

Engage
Page 39

Objective
To understand how values are formed in the family

Pray
Psalm 128

Focus
Discuss the meaning of "walking in the ways of God."

Discover
Identify and explain various kinds of values.

Teach
Page 40

Objective
To examine the positive influence we can have on others

Focus
Catholics Believe: Being a "living stone" in the Family of God

Explore
Read, discuss and summarize the impact of peer pressure and its positive and negative influence on individuals as they mature.
Growing in Virtue: Responsible use of positive peer pressure

Connect
Rating values and the pressure one feels to assimilate that value.

Apply
Page 42

Objective
To describe ways in which our values are put into action

Focus
Explain a personal influential proverb or saying.

Discover
Catholic Family Album: Saint Hilary of Poitiers

Integrate
Describe ways to put specific good values into action.

Pray
Popular or favorite hymn, easy for all to participate

Reviewing Unit 1
Summarize and review the content from both lessons.

Vocabulary Preview

Peer Pressure—influence of others, especially those closest to us, like our friends

Perseverance—the act of continuing with patient effort despite obstacles

Responsibility—the character strength of being dependable, putting care for others and the world around us into action

Value—comes from the Latin word *valēre*, meaning "to be of worth"

Materials Needed

▶ writing paper
▶ pens, pencils
▶ art supplies
▶ influential proverb or saying
▶ Bible
▶ Lesson 2 Activity Masters

Call to Prayer

Jesus, guide us all as we seek to discover who we are and whom we should become. Be the strong, true light that helps all young people to grow in maturity. Amen.

Values and Virtues

Living Treasures

Carlos was surfing around on the Internet. He stumbled on a site entitled "The Treasure Trove." The site was one big auction. People were trying to sell their attic, basement or garage treasures to the highest bidder. Carlos was curious. So, he stayed on the site for a while to see what was happening.

Each time an item was brought up for sale, the seller would tell what a wonderful treasure the item was. One woman was selling her wedding dress. It had been in her family for four generations. A teenager was selling his collection of hockey cards. An elderly gentleman was selling a walking stick that had a carving of a camel's head for a handle.

After each item was auctioned, the following words would pop up on the computer screen: "What is your greatest treasure? Turn that treasure into cash!" Carlos shut down his Internet connection. "If I really treasured something, why would I want to sell it?" he said to himself.

Values are living treasures. Your personal values are the actions and the attitudes you hold most dear. You have acquired your personal values from many sources. Your family is an important source of your values.

What actions and attitudes did you get from your family? Maybe your father taught you perseverance. From his example, you learned never to give up on a task, even a very difficult one. Maybe your mother taught you the value of being honest in all things. Or maybe your grandparents taught you to be generous and forgiving by the way they always treated you.

> **This lesson will help you to:**
> - **explore** how values are formed in the family.
> - **examine** the positive influence we can have on others by living our values.
> - **decide** ways in which we can put our values into action.

 What values do you hold most dear and why?

Values and Virtues **15**

Teaching Tip

Family Values: Identifying specific values held dear by a person's family might be difficult without putting it in context or could be intimidating for the individual person to share. Therefore, in discussing family values, clearly communicate from the beginning that there is no judgment being made concerning the specific values identified for anyone's family. Point out that our actions typically communicate what we find valuable or important. Listing family values helps individuals make more sense of what has been influential and important in their lives. Values guide us to make informed decisions about what is held to be important.

> **Objective**
>
> *To understand how values are formed in the family*

Pray

Open the lesson by praying Psalm 128 seeking God's blessing upon our families.

Focus

Discuss with students Psalm 128:1b asking them what they think are examples of "walking in the ways of God."

Discover

► Ask students to rank their belongings currently with them, according to the value each has for them.

► Discuss the reasons for the value or importance certain possessions have.

► Read "Living Treasures." Allow students to ask questions about the reading.

► Group students to discuss the question: "What values do you hold most dear and why?" Have one student from each group report to the class the group's response to the question.

► Time permitting, categorize the groups' responses according to the kind of value represented. For example, "Doing what is right" is a value held dear and would be categorized as a "Moral Value." Create categories appropriate to group responses.

Objective

To examine the positive influence we can have on others

Focus

Read aloud Catholics Believe. Explain that how we act also affects the Church, the Family of God. Inquire: What does it mean to be a "living stone?"

Explore

▶ Invite students to play a version of Simon Says. Have students take turns being "Simon." Direct each "Simon" to have the others pantomime specific actions that depict a value that contributes to family life, for example, generosity, forgiveness, etc.

▶ Discuss the game as an example of peer pressure; is it positive or negative?

▶ Have students quietly read "A City Built Under Pressure." As the class reads aloud, pause for students to react or ask questions. Then have them read the rest of the text.

▶ Inquire: How did you feel when playing the Simon Says game? How were you influenced by the "pressure" you might have felt?

▶ Discuss the example from the reading on the pressure to say yes to what is true, beautiful and good.

Catholics Believe

The Church is often called the building of God. Christ is the cornerstone, and we are the "living stones" here on earth built into it. We are called to contribute to the building of the New Jerusalem, the Holy City, in which the family of God dwells.

A City Built Under Pressure

Like Carlos, you have learned and are learning values from your family. When you put these values into practice, you contribute to the building of a family, a school community, a neighborhood, a country and, yes, the world God created.

When you say yes to what is true, beautiful and good, you are using the gift of free will. God gave you this gift for that purpose. You are also demonstrating maturity and responsibility. God has created us to live with more freedom, passion and joy than most people imagine.

What would it be like living in a city where people, filled by God's life, love their way through life? Where everyone speaks the truth? Where people work hard and persevere in their duties and responsibilities?

Imagine a world in which all people of every walk of life are sincere, generous, humble, kind, patient and funny. As God's family, we join with Jesus and work toward building this kind of world—a world Jesus named the Kingdom of God. We contribute to the building of the Kingdom by saying yes to God and by putting into practice the values Jesus lived and proclaimed.

Pressure

We will face challenges when we commit ourselves to saying yes to God. But the good news is we have been given the gifts of the Holy Spirit to successfully handle the pressure these challenges bring our way.

 Think about the kind of pressure you experience when saying yes to God.

This does not deny or ignore that sometimes these pressures are negative. There are temptations or sins in life. Yet when we focus primarily on saying yes to what is true, beautiful and good, we are also saying no to that which prevents us from creating this God-centered city, the Kingdom announced by Jesus.

Pressure from our friends, or peer pressure, is not always pressure to do wrong. Often pressure from our friends can

16   Values and Virtues

Teaching Tip

Displaying Values: Set up a table display of various items that represent values, for example, a crucifix (Catholic faith), an American flag (citizenship), wedding ring (marriage), a fake $10 bill (money), photos of family and friends (relationships), toy (fun), etc. Use this display or individual objects to elicit reactions on how objects symbolize or represent what we value. Explain that by surrounding ourselves with these objects, we communicate what we value. They can also remind us of what is important to our life. In this last way, "objects of value" can be a positive peer pressure.

challenge us to live by our values. Consider the following example:

> Marian and Jill were online when they saw a post from someone in their class. This person promised pictures that would embarrass Cindy, one of their classmates. "Let's look at them!" Marian suggested. Jill replied, "I don't even want to see them, Marian. Let's text Cindy and let her know what we discovered." Marian agreed, "You're right. We need to let Cindy and her parents know what is going on."

Your desire for belonging is strong. It might have been easier for Marian and Jill just to give in, look at the pictures of Cindy and pass them on to others. Facing that and other temptations is not always easy. This is precisely why we need one another. We need to help each other, even "pressure" each other, to say yes to what is true, beautiful and good for the sake of building a God-centered city, the Kingdom of God.

Growing in Virtue

The virtue of **counsel**, or right judgment, is also one of the Seven Gifts of the Holy Spirit. Choosing to love your way through life means using the gift of your free will to say yes to what is true, beautiful and good. Good judgment also helps us to respond to peer pressure in a way that enables us to live our values.

"Pressure Gauge"

On the line write the highest value you believe people your age have. Draw the gauge's needle to rate how much pressure you feel to have that value. Then describe how you handle that pressure.

Highest Value for Your Age: | **How do you handle it?**

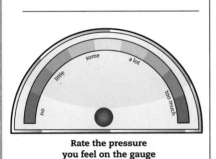

Rate the pressure
you feel on the gauge

Values and Virtues 17

▶ Have students name some of the peer pressure that they experience. Have them practice handling this pressure in positive ways, offering a positive response to negative pressure. Remind students that they have the right to say no to unwanted pressure from anyone. Encourage them to speak to a trusted adult if they have concerns about the pressures they experience.

▶ Read Growing in Virtue. Inquire: How is positive pressure a sign of maturity? What qualities would a person need to say yes to what is true, beautiful and good?

Connect

▶ Pair students to identify the qualities they have that would help them say yes to what is true, beautiful and good.

▶ Then have the pairs brainstorm a list of high values they think people their age have. Allow time for the pairs to discuss how these values might produce positive or negative peer pressure.

▶ Have students complete the activity on the page. If needed, have them finish the activity at home with their family.

▶ Time permitting, research the twelve Gifts of the Holy Spirit as signs of the Spirit dwelling within us and aiding us in our actions.

Extending the Lesson

Using Activity Master 2A: Use the Activity Master "Seals and Mottos." This activity helps students graphically design an image that highlights a particular value. Two state seals and mottos are provided as examples.

Popular Slogans: Have students write parodies of current popular advertisements that give negative messages. The purpose of the parody is to show the foolishness of falling for the negative peer pressure that the advertisement tries to exert on us. Give the option to write a serious advertisement or slogan that promotes saying yes to what is true, beautiful and good. Suggest that students create a graphic design of the advertisement or slogan for public display.

Objective

To describe ways in which our values are put into action

Focus

Display a large sign with a saying, proverb or maxim that has value for you. Explain how these words have influenced you.

Discover

Read the Catholic Family Album box. Ask: What guided St. Hilary of Poitiers in his life? *(Scripture, Church teachings, love for God)* Explain that when we put our faith into action, we communicate values.

Integrate

▶ Read "Putting Good Values in Action." Respond to any questions students may have about completing the activity on the page.

▶ Have students complete the activity.

▶ Time permitting, have students research quotes, sayings, lyrics, etc. that might help them recall the important values in their lives so they will act on them.

Pray

Invite students to sing a popular or favorite hymn for prayer. Be sure the song is easy enough to sing for all to participate.

Catholic Family Album

Saint Hilary of Poitiers (315–367) was a good communicator of the faith. He believed that all Christians have the responsibility to put their faith into action. Hilary did this in many ways. He studied the Bible and clearly communicated the teachings of the Bible to help the Church clarify her teachings, especially on the Holy Trinity. He wrote many hymns and promoted the use of songs to joyfully express the faith. He desired to excite in the hearts of others a love for God. He was appointed bishop of Poitiers in France. Today, St. Hilary is honored as a Father of the Church. His feast day is celebrated on January 14.

Putting Good Values in Action

A virtue is the good habit of acting according to what is moral and good. Your values become virtues when you act on them. For example, Jill and Marian acted on their values. They refused to look at the photos of Cindy and told her and her parents about the pictures that someone was about to post on the Internet.

Your family's actions show the values it holds to be most important. If hospitality were valued in your family, then you would act in a just way inviting guests and providing a welcoming environment for them. These actions intentionally reflect the good values of your family.

Look at the list of values in the chart below. Select three and describe how you will put them into action.

VIRTUES: VALUES IN ACTION

Generosity	Kindness	Sincerity
Patience	Common Sense	Hospitality

Value/Virtue 1:
I will

_____

_____

Value/Virtue 2:
I will

_____

_____

Value/Virtue 3:
I will

_____

_____

18   Values and Virtues

Extending the Lesson

Using Activity Master 2B: Use the Activity Master "You Be the Judge." This activity helps students analyze and evaluate situations in which peer pressure might influence decisions. Use this activity to help students become more aware of the influence on not only their family and friends, but also on the media and society at large.

Spiritual Influence: Researching patron saints can be a way of using positive peer pressure in a spiritual way. The writings of the saints can also serve to inspire us to say yes to what is true, beautiful and good. Their lives serve as witness to the happiness one finds in living the Great Commandment.

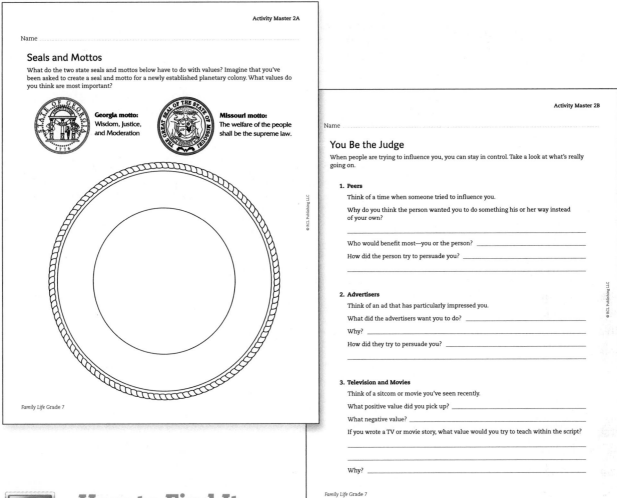

Activity Master 2A

Name ....

Seals and Mottos

What do the two state seals and mottos below have to do with values? Imagine that you've been asked to create a seal and motto for a newly established planetary colony. What values do you think are most important?

Georgia motto:
Wisdom, Justice, and Moderation

Missouri motto:
The welfare of the people shall be the supreme law.

Family Life Grade 7

Activity Master 2B

Name ....

You Be the Judge

When people are trying to influence you, you can stay in control. Take a look at what's really going on.

1. Peers

Think of a time when someone tried to influence you.

Why do you think the person wanted you to do something his or her way instead of your own?

_____

Who would benefit most—you or the person? _____

How did the person try to persuade you? _____

_____

2. Advertisers

Think of an ad that has particularly impressed you.

What did the advertisers want you to do? _____

Why? _____

How did they try to persuade you? _____

_____

3. Television and Movies

Think of a sitcom or movie you've seen recently.

What positive value did you pick up? _____

What negative value? _____

If you wrote a TV or movie story, what value would you try to teach within the script?

_____

_____

Why? _____

Family Life Grade 7

How to Find It
How to Use It

Step 1: Click & Select

Go to RCLBFamilyLife.com
Click on the link for activities.
Then select the activity master you need.

Step 2: Print & Copy

Print each activity master in advance.
Then copy enough for everyone in the class.

Step 3: Share & Discuss

Once students have completed the activity,
have them share and discuss their responses.

Summary

▶ Ask the students to read through the Summary section.

▶ Invite them to ask questions about any points that are not clear to them.

▶ Make sure to expand on any points that were perhaps touched on only lightly during class time.

Thinking It Through

▶ Have students answer all three questions on the page.

▶ Assign each student a number from one through three.

▶ Have students share with the class their answer to the question that corresponds to their assigned number.

Matching It Up

Use this matching section to help the students identify the appropriate definition or description of a key concept, term or person from the unit.

Name ....

Summary

Remember what you have learned in each of the lessons in God's Gift of Family.

LESSON 1: Family Relationships

• Your birth order or being an only child affects your relationship with others.

• Both the good habit, or virtue, of compassion and the skill of listening help a person communicate effectively.

• Conflict is sometimes a part of family life. Learning the skills for resolving conflict peacefully is helpful for better communication.

LESSON 2: Values and Virtues

• Many of your values are formed in your family, and influence your actions.

• Responsible use of positive peer pressure is a sign of maturity and demonstrates respect for others.

• Putting good values into action results in virtuous living. Your Catholic faith helps you practice Christian virtues.

Thinking It Through

1. What are some ways you practice good communication with your family members?

_____

_____

2. What techniques do you use to resolve conflict peacefully?

_____

_____

3. How are your values influenced by your faith?

_____

_____

Matching It Up

On each line, write the letter of the description in Column B that best goes with the term in Column A.

A

1. ___E___ Blended Family

2. ___C___ Compassion

3. ___A___ Listening

4. ___D___ Personal Values

5. ___B___ Virtue

B

A. Part of good communication, paying attention to what is being said

B. Habit of acting according to what is moral and good

C. Helps you discover something about another's attitudes and needs

D. Actions and attitudes that you hold most dear

E. When adults with children from a previous marriage enter into a new marriage

Unit 1 Review   19

Teaching Tip

Parent Letter: Send a letter home to the parents. Tell them to ask their child about what they have learned in unit 1. Encourage the parents to use the Family Time pages at home before and after the unit lessons.

Unit Reviews: These unit review sections do not have to be completed as formal testing or assessments. They are designed to assist students in recalling the essential content of each lesson under their common unit theme. This is an opportunity for either the classroom setting or as a take-home assignment. You can informally assess student progress for each unit as you proceed. Be sure to provide a clear summary of the content in your own words before proceeding to the next unit.

REVIEWING UNIT 1

Name...

Recalling Key Concepts

Circle the T if the statement is true. Circle the F if the statement is false.

1. Values are passed on primarily by families.   (T)   F
2. Christian living is shaped by the values of society.   T   (F)
3. Peer pressure is only negative and always leads one to sin.   T   (F)
4. Compassion means "feeling for" or "sorrow for."   T   (F)
5. Your own and other people's expectations of you are often affected by your family birth order.   (T)   F

Fill in the missing words in these sentences.

6. **HONESTY** .... is the virtue that says to tell the truth and to keep only the things that belong to you.

7. The .... **FAMILY** .... is your first community.

8. The Church is sometimes called the building of God. Christians are its " .... **LIVING** .... **STONES** .... "

9. Catholics look to .... **SCRIPTURE** .... and the teachings of the Church to guide us in making good moral decisions.

10. Messengers of God are also known as .... **ANGELS** ....

Working Together

In small groups name and talk about conflicts that families might commonly experience. Have your group choose one conflict and decide how best to resolve it. Act out the conflict and how it might be handled to resolve it peacefully. Have each small group share its conflict and the way you resolved it with the class. See if anyone else in the class has ideas for other ways to resolve the conflict.

20   Unit 1 Review

Recalling Key Concepts

▶ Use this section to help the students be able to accurately recall the key concepts from the unit.

▶ For the true and false section, you can have students correct any false statements.

▶ To help with the fill-in-the-blank section, you might want to provide a word bank on the board.

Working Together

▶ Choose a project that best fits the need and abilities of your students, as well as your time schedule.

▶ Time permitting, have students complete the unit assessment individually or as a class; otherwise encourage them to complete it at home.

▶ End the unit with a prayer.

Teaching Tip

Flash-Point Issues: Consider using flash-point issues as concerns for an advice panel of students, such as a student council, to address. Flash-point issues might include gossip, disloyalty among friends, fairness, etc. Have each of the parties in conflict present their views and seek advice from the student panel. The student panel is to reach a decision based on values found in Catholic teachings.

God's Gift of Self

Background

"So the very sacramentality of creation, the sacramentality of the world was revealed in a way, in man created in the image of God. By means of his corporality, his masculinity and femininity, man becomes a visible sign of the economy of truth and love, which has its source in God himself and which was revealed already in the mystery of creation" (Pope John Paul II, General Audience, February 20, 1980).

THE HUMAN PERSON IS ONE OF THE GREATEST miracles of creation. We live in a time when scientists are discovering many of the amazing complexities that resulted in our being here on Earth. Encourage your students to appreciate the richness of their personhood, especially as they mature into being responsible adults.

Unfortunately we live in a society that tends to reduce the mystery of the human person. Pope John Paul II in the above passage emphasizes that God is the source of everyone's existence. That means that we all belong to God. As the Church teaches, we come from God and we will return to God. God is our beginning and our final destination.

EVERY PERSON POSSESSES SACRED DIGNITY. THIS IS one of the most essential aspects of being a person. There are no exceptions to this bold assertion. Further, God loves each person in the full knowledge of each person's uniqueness. God loves us as we are! Through each person, God makes known some special aspect of his own self. We are all valued by God as his children. The Apostle John reminds us "See what love the Father

has bestowed on us that we may be called the children of God" (1 John 3:1).

Spend some quiet time reflecting on your own inherent worth. This is not easy because we tend to judge ourselves through the eyes of others or through values that come from our limited cultural perspective. Try to imagine how much God loves you. Because we are so loved, we do well to take care of ourselves. In degrading or damaging our personhood through harmful substances or thoughts, we neglect the goodness of God that is embedded within us.

GOD CREATED HUMANKIND MALE AND FEMALE. "In creating the human race 'male and female' God gives man and woman an equal dignity, endowing them with the inalienable rights and responsibilities proper to the human person" (*Familiaris Consortio* 22). Men and women are complementary. There are gifts or qualities that men do not naturally possess that are more commonly found in women. In turn, other gifts are more prevalent in men than in women. There is a balance and a complementarity in the natural sharing of gifts, inclinations and qualities of the sexes. Complementary genders are a gift from a wise Creator.

Additional Background

Catechism of the Catholic Church:
§§ 1763–1764, 1767, 1769

The stereotyping of genders undermines the divine plan of Creation. Sexual stereotypes standardize narrow views of men and women and foster false ideas and unhealthy attitudes. Stereotypes can lead to oppressive relationships and even social structures that are sinful.

For Reflection

Read and reflect on the following:

We must remember how adolescents . . . are preoccupied and at times disturbed not only by the problems of self-identity, . . . They also have problems in accepting themselves and their bodies" (The Truth and Meaning in Human Sexuality *106*).

▸ How is the uniqueness of each family member in my family acknowledged and celebrated?

▸ What might I do to be aware of stereotyping in my class? What might I do to foster the dignity and equality of every young person in the class?

Child Safety

Adolescents are at high risk for sexual abuse because of their strong need to be accepted. Taking advantage of their mental, emotional and psychological immaturity, abusers often look for teens who have few friends and inadequate support systems and then "groom" them using compliments and promises of companionship. In this way, many adolescent victims of sexual abuse are tricked into believing that they are involved in a loving, healthy "adult" sexual relationship. The lessons in this unit will help the students recognize and avoid such sexual grooming.

 Family Time

Partnering with the Family

This is a good time for the family to look at its own life and examine how much each family member contributes to the family's prayer life. Thank God for each family member, noting their special qualities. Encourage parents to discuss with their child how each family member is shown respect. Suggest that they use the Family Time pages that begin each unit to discuss the topics covered in both lessons.

LESSON 3 PLANNER

Goal: To examine spiritual maturity in light of the changes that test one's resiliency during puberty

Engage
Page 49

Objective
To identify different ways in which a person grows in maturity

Family Time
Ensure that each student tears out their Family Time page to complete at home.

Pray
Learning from Jesus about spiritual maturity

Focus
Define through discussion what it means to be mature.

Discover
Identify and explain the four facets of maturity.

Teach
Page 50

Objective
To understand some of the changes during puberty

Focus
Catholics Believe: Spiritual maturity

Explore
Read, discuss and summarize the important changes during puberty as related to growing in maturity.
Growing in Virtue: Resilience in practicing fortitude

Connect
Describe yourself using all four facets of maturity.

Apply
Page 52

Objective
To discern more about God's calling as related to growing in maturity

Focus
Discuss the healthy skill of self-acceptance.

Discover
Catholic Family Album: Saint Gertrude the Great

Integrate
Respond to various questions that help identity the person God is calling you to be.

Pray
Psalm 139

Vocabulary Preview

Adolescence—a stage of life between childhood and adulthood. The word comes from the Latin, *adolescens*, which means "growing up" or "growing toward."

Endocrine System—a collection of glands that make hormones that regulate body growth, reproductive development and metabolism

Maturity—the process through which one realizes their full potential

Resilience—the ability to adjust to change, or the capacity to survive and recover from change; a character strength developed through the exercise of fortitude

Materials Needed

▶ writing paper
▶ pens, pencils
▶ art supplies
▶ Bible
▶ Lesson 3 Activity Masters

Call to Prayer

Jesus, guide us all as we seek to discover who we are and whom we should become. Be the strong, true light that helps all young people to grow in maturity. Amen.

Identity

Heading Toward Maturity

During adolescence, your brain reaches adult size and weight. Your ability to think and to reason increases. You begin to look at things in new ways and make decisions more independently. Your memory skills improve, and you are becoming better able to understand someone else's point of view.

You may also be experiencing your emotions more strongly. Emotions are natural and are caused by changes taking place in your body. Being aware of how you feel and naming your emotions will enable you to better deal with the changes you are experiencing.

During adolescence, your ability to think abstractly will increase. Abstract thinking helps you make connections or understand relationships between ideas. This means that you are maturing in your understanding of things and are moving beyond concrete thinking or beyond your immediate tangible experiences. For example, you are becoming more aware of yourself as independent from others. You are maturing in your understanding of yourself and the world around you.

You are also maturing spiritually. Spiritual maturity is rooted in trust. A spiritually mature person trusts God, in good and difficult times. Spiritual maturity is a journey of faith. Just as your vision of the world changes with age, so does your understanding of God. The Gospel, Church teachings, prayer, sacramental celebrations and faith-filled people help you along your journey toward spiritual maturity.

> **This lesson will help you to:**
> - **explore** the different ways you are maturing.
> - **understand** the changes during puberty.
> - **affirm** that your identity is about your whole person, body and soul.

 Who or what in your life helps you to be more mature in how you think, feel and behave?

Identity **23**

Teaching Tip

A Passage into Maturity: Take time to discuss with students about various rites of passage that mark a passage to maturity among young people. These rites of passage could be cultural, ethnic or religious. For example, in the United States, the age of eighteen marks a point of maturity resulting in being able to vote. In the Jewish culture, a bar mitzvah (for boys) or a bat mitzvah (for girls) is a celebration of maturity. Similarly, in the Hispanic cultures, a Quinceñera marks the fifteenth birthday for a young girl. Encourage students to discover more about their family's cultural and religious rites of passage into maturity. Ask students why they think it is important to celebrate a milestone of maturity.

> ### Objective
> To identify different ways in which a person grows in maturity

Pray

Open the lesson with a prayer seeking guidance from Jesus as we mature spiritually.

Focus

Have students debate if a person is ever completely mature. Be sure that they clearly define "maturity" in all aspects, especially spiritually.

Discover

- ► Read "Heading Toward Maturity." Provide time for students to ask questions about the reading.

- ► Identify on the board the four dimensions of maturity: physical, mental, emotional and spiritual.

- ► Invite students to list a series of "I can" statements for each dimension of maturity.

- ► Discuss how their "I can" statements reflect self-awareness. Inquire: How can you show spiritual maturity in your relationship with God?

- ► Time permitting, have each student identify a person whom they admire because of their maturity. Explain that maturity, especially spiritual maturity, continues for a lifetime.

Objective

To understand some of the changes during puberty

Focus

▶ Read aloud the Catholics Believe box. Inquire: Why is being open to accept and act upon God's grace a sign of spiritual maturity?

▶ Read aloud Wisdom 4:8–9. Explain that understanding and doing God's will is a sign of spiritual maturity.

Explore

▶ Conduct a blind poll by asking students these or similar questions: (1) Have you noticed recently in yourself a growth spurt? (2) Are you ever embarrassed by some of the changes you are experiencing? (3) Do you feel glad sometimes about growing toward adulthood?

▶ Report the results of the blind poll, noting similar responses.

▶ Have students quietly read, "Change in Motion." Discuss the different kinds of "growth spurts" that students are experiencing.

▶ Have students discuss examples of mature and immature behavior. Include all four facets of maturity. Note how these spurts show that they can handle more of the same kinds of changes.

Catholics Believe

Christian maturity is not limited by the age of our body nor to intellectual ability. Spiritual maturity means becoming more like Jesus in being open to accept and respond to the free and unmerited grace of God (CCC 1308).

Change in Motion

If you look around your classroom, you will notice that there can be a great deal of difference in the level of physical maturity among your classmates. The reason for that is simple. Everyone goes through stages of maturity, including physical maturity, at a different pace.

God created us in such a way that our physical growth is determined by the endocrine system. This system is made up of glands that work together to keep a body healthy. Heredity and diet influence the working of our endocrine system.

The endocrine glands secrete chemicals called hormones into the bloodstream. The word *hormone* comes from a Greek word that means "to set in motion." God has set in motion within your body a means of growing that is essentially the same for everyone, but at a pace unique to each individual.

Hormones act as messengers throughout your body. Your body produces about thirty different hormones. One of the most active ones in your life right now is nicknamed the growth hormone. The growth hormone, or *somatotropin*, sets body growth in motion. During adolescence, this hormone is released at an increased rate and thus growth spurts result.

 Think about the different kinds of growth and maturity that you have recently experienced.

It is not only your body but also your whole self that is undergoing amazing growth at this stage of your life. The amazing growth occurring in you and your friends is happening physically, mentally, emotionally and spiritually. Through puberty, you might recognize how God has created you to be resilient. This means that as you mature, you grow in your ability to handle more challenges. While hormones help your body be resilient, your mind and will can help the rest of you think and choose to be strong. Just as your body needs exercise to maintain healthy growth so does your mind and "spirit." You need to practice the virtue

24 Identity

Teaching Tip

Sexual Grooming: Over time, predators "groom" their victims through compliments and companionship. Here are possible grooming scenarios to share with the youth:

- An adult sends you e-mails that praise your looks and abilities, and then suggests that you choose a time to come to their home.

- A relative visits your home. They sit close enough to touch you while watching TV and compliment you greatly. You are invited that evening to their room to look at some cool pictures.

- Your brother's friend, a high school junior, visits frequently and likes to hang out with you. He jokes around, tickles you and likes to wrestle you on the floor.

of fortitude through resilience, to stay healthy mentally, emotionally and spiritually.

God created you as a whole person, body and soul. Your soul is the spiritual part of you that never dies. And he desires for you to know more fully who you are. With God's grace, you can and will grow in maturity.

What is even more incredible about all this growth is that through all of this change, God has given you the ability to come to know yourself better. For example, intellectually as you study the physical sciences and all the body systems that God designed, you will be able to apply that knowledge to understanding more about how you can stay healthy and safe. Spiritually, as you mature in faith, you will be able to reflect and discern more about your relationship with God.

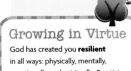

Growing in Virtue

God has created you **resilient** in all ways: physically, mentally, emotionally and spiritually. Practicing the virtue of fortitude, or courage, exercises both your mind and will to know and choose to do what is right in seeking true happiness.

"Looking in the Mirror"

Find some quiet time to look at yourself in a mirror. Write down who you see yourself to be at that moment. Describe all aspects of your personhood.

Activity

Physically I am
_____
_____

Mentally I am
_____
_____

Emotionally I am
_____
_____

Spiritually I am
_____
_____

Identity 25

Extending the Lesson

Using Activity Master 3A: Use the Activity Master "Growing with Style." This activity helps students work through some of the discomforts and confusions of puberty by asking questions related to clothing, design and style. This activity expands the Teach Activity in drawing out a deeper connection between concepts taught and decisions made in their own lives.

Identity Panel: Invite a panel of Catholic adults to talk with boys and girls separately and together about maturing into adulthood. The adults are to focus on how they dealt with their experience of the four dimensions of maturity. Catholic adults might include a representative of each vocational state of life, namely a priest, a religious, a single person and a married couple.

▶ Introduce the concept of "sexual grooming" (see Teaching Tip). How might teens be manipulated by someone? That's what sexual grooming is. Discuss prevention and rejection of such manipulation.

▶ Explain that normal adults should befriend other adults not children or teenagers.

▶ Be prepared to talk with students about appropriate behavior between sexes at their age (group outings, group hugs), but keep the conversation appropriate as well. Remind students that they can say no to any unwanted touches.

▶ Read the Growing in Virtue box. Explain that with God's grace and practicing the cardinal virtue of fortitude, a person becomes morally and spiritually stronger, able to handle more.

Connect

▶ Explain that just as physical maturity provides physical signs, spiritual maturity has spiritual signs. Invite the students to quietly reflect on their personal relationship with God. Inquire: What spiritual signs do you have in your relationship with God?

▶ Have students complete the activity on the page.

▶ Time permitting, invite students to discuss how struggles in life can help us become stronger. Use a sports analogy or Jesus as a spiritual healer to point to how resilient God has created us.

APPLY

Objective

To discern more about God's calling as related to growing in maturity

Focus

Discuss what it means to accept yourself as God created you. Explain that a healthy acceptance of our weaknesses, for example, means being realistic about our limitations as well as our potential.

Discover

Read the Catholic Family Album box. Ask: How did St. Gertrude show her spiritual maturity? *(She shared the divine joy she experienced in seeking to love God.)*

Integrate

▶ Read "Identify Yourself." Allow time for students to quietly review the questions before they respond.

▶ To provide an atmosphere necessary for reflection, request silence or play appropriate music.

▶ Have students quietly respond to the questions on the page. Time permitting, ask volunteers to share a few of their responses with the class.

Pray

Conclude the lesson by having students prayerfully read aloud Psalm 139.

Catholic Family Album

Saint Gertrude the Great (1256–1302) used her mental, emotional and spiritual gifts to come to a deeper understanding of herself, others and God. Gertrude, who was exceptionally smart, spent much of her time studying literature and philosophy as well as copying manuscripts by hand. At the age of twenty-six she received a mystical vision from Christ. After this experience, Gertrude spent the rest of her life pursuing a deeper understanding of God and guided others on their spiritual journey through her advice and writings.

What I will do!

To work toward achieving this goal, I will

Identify Yourself

Throughout your life, you will hear one question perhaps more than almost any other, "Who are you?" Most often you will identify yourself by telling your name.

The ability to discover, appreciate and value yourself as God created you is called self-acceptance. In the years ahead, you will grow in your understanding of yourself, both your strengths and weaknesses. Learn to be realistic about your weaknesses and to build on your strengths.

Spend a few moments answering the following questions, and come to know yourself better.

1. Three words that best describe me are

2. My proudest achievement is

3. What I most like about myself is

4. The thing that gives me the most confidence is

5. If I could change one thing about myself, I would

6. My favorite way to pray is

7. My biggest fear about the future is

8. My favorite saint is

9. The thing that makes me most sad is

10. A goal I have for my future is

26 Identity

Extending the Lesson

Using Activity Master 3B: Use the Activity Master "The Magic Triangle." This activity provides instructions on how to make a standing triangle out of a piece of paper. The point of the lesson is to learn from our mistakes.

Fully Alive: Write on the board this saying by St. Irenaeus of Lyons: "The glory of God is man fully alive." Invite students to change "man" to "me" or their proper name and say it aloud. Then discuss as a class what it means to be "fully alive" and how that connects with the "glory of God." Conclude by inviting responses to the question: How does your dependence on God affect the way in which you choose to live?

Activity Master 3A

Name

Growing with Style

No doubt about it—puberty has its discomforts. But it's also a great time to discover your special style. What it's not is a time to go on hold and wait for your teen years to pass. Use these questions to think about your particular style.

1. If it were possible, would you like to throw out your present wardrobe, and dress a totally different way? If your answer is yes, what would your clothes be like? If your answer is no, why do you like your present wardrobe?

2. Do you think the image you project to your friends is the real you? If your answer is yes, write a sentence that defines your style. If your answer is no, what could you do to show them who you really are?

3. Picture yourself in your dream career. What's your style: decisive executive, artistic genius, gifted homemaker, laid-back wilderness guide, dedicated scientist—or something else? How can you work on building that style right now?

4. How do you think an adult can "grow old gracefully"?

How do you think you can get through puberty with style?

Family Life Grade 7

© RCL Publishing LLC

Activity Master 3B

Name

The Magic Triangle

You can use mistakes as a cop-out, or use them to learn. As you try this project, you may make some mistakes. How will you use them? (Can you ask for help when you need it?)

1. Fold a sheet of 8½″ x 11″ typing paper diagonally from one corner so the edges meet.
2. Cut off the end to make a square measuring 8½″ x 8½″.
3. Fold both edges inward so they just meet the middle fold.
4. The project should look like this.
5. Fold upward on the dotted line so the project looks like this.
6. Fold up the two corners on the dotted lines. (The two edges shouldn't quite meet the middle fold. There should be about ⅛″ between them.)
7. The project should look like this.
8. Fold up on the dotted line.
9. The project should look like this.
10. Fold up the two corners on the dotted lines. (Again, the two edges shouldn't meet the middle fold.)
11. The project should look like this (a bit lumpy).
12. Fold the whole thing in half, so it looks like this. (Don't worry if the middle fold tears a little.)
13. Hold the fold together while you place the project on your desk like this.
14. As it unfolds, the Magic Triangle will rise by itself to a standing position!

Family Life Grade 7

© RCL Publishing LLC

How to Find It
How to Use It

Step 1: Click & Select

Go to RCLBFamilyLife.com
Click on the link for activities.
Then select the activity master you need.

Step 2: Print & Copy

Print each activity master in advance.
Then copy enough for everyone in the class.

Step 3: Share & Discuss

Once students have completed the activity,
have them share and discuss their responses.

Goal: To examine God's plan in creating complementary genders to help a person accept and appreciate their gender

Engage
Page 55

Objective
To identify the major aspects of gender

Pray
Genesis 1:26–27

Focus
Facilitate a discussion on gender association.

Discover
Identify and explain the three major aspects of gender.

Teach
Page 56

Objective
To understand the complementarity between genders

Focus
Identify careers as potentially exclusive to a particular gender.

Explore
Read, discuss and summarize the importance of complementarity of genders and problems of gender stereotyping.
Catholics Believe: Society depends on the complementarity between husband and wife.
Growing in Virtue: Accepting and appreciating one's gender

Connect
Critique a movie or TV show's portrayal of gender differences.

Apply
Page 58

Objective
To explore attitudes about being created as male or female

Focus
Ephesians 5:21–33

Discover
Catholic Family Album: Saint Paul of Tarsus

Integrate
Evaluate personal attitudes about what it means to be male or female.

Pray
Prayer on qualities

Reviewing Unit 2
Summarize and review the content from both lessons.

Vocabulary Preview

Complementarity—to live with and for each other as equal in dignity, helping each other according to God's plan for the two genders

Diligence—in the context of sexual identity, the steadfast attention and appreciation of one's gender

Sexual Identity—sexuality; everything about a person that relates to the person as being created either male or female

Stereotype—erroneous ideas or false preconceived notions about an individual

Materials Needed

▸ writing paper
▸ pens, pencils
▸ art supplies
▸ popular movie or television show
▸ Bible
▸ Lesson 4 Activity Masters

Call to Prayer

God, you have created males and females in your image and likeness. Thank you for the beautiful gift of our sexuality. Amen.

Gender

Male and Female He Created Them

The Book of Genesis has a very simple verse that tells of the crowning wonder of God's love. "God created man in his image; / in the divine image he created him; / male and female he created them" (Genesis 1:27).

God created human beings with the gift of human sexuality, or gender. Sexuality is the gift of being a man or a woman, a boy or a girl. The word *gender* refers to a person's sexual identity as male or female. There are three aspects of a person's gender: physical, psychological and spiritual.

1. **Physical:** The most obvious aspect of gender is related to our body. This is determined at the moment of conception when chromosomes from parents are joined. If a Y chromosome from the father joins an X from the mother, the result would be XY, and the gender of the baby is male. Otherwise X chromosomes from both parents would join and the baby is female.

2. **Psychological:** The way you view yourself as male or female is called your psychological gender. Parents and others help to affirm the gender of boys and girls.

3. **Spiritual:** Our capacity to love and be in relationships with God and others is affected by our gender. As an image of the power and tenderness of God, he created both men and women with differences that balance and complete one another.

Men and women need to accept their sexual identity. Through our sexuality we express and share our life and love most intimately with and for others. The only proper place for intimate sexual activity is within a lifelong marriage between a man and a woman.

As you develop, your gender is expressed in a series of changes. If these changes embarrass or worry you, be patient with yourself. Share your feelings with your parents, another trusted adult, or even an older sibling who has been through the same things already.

> This lesson will help you to:
> - **explore** the meaning of gender.
> - **understand** that males and females complement each other.
> - **affirm** your gender.

 In what ways have you learned to appreciate and value your own gender?

Gender 27

Objective

To identify the major aspects of gender

Pray

Open the lesson by reading Genesis 1:26–27 reflecting on God's plan for both males and females.

Focus

Have students list items for purchase that are exclusive to each gender. Facilitate a discussion about their lists. Inquire: How did you choose the items?

Discover

▶ Read "Male and Female He Created Them." Allow time for students to ask questions about the reading.

▶ Divide the class into three groups; assign each one of the three aspects. Have each group provide examples of that aspect for each gender; for example, psychological: boys are more aggressive.

▶ Time permitting, discuss whether or not their examples are factual or stereotypical.

Teaching Tip

Child Safety Tips for Parents: Share this important information with the children's parents or guardians:

- Friendships outside the home are very important. Know your child's friends: who they are, where they spend their time and what they do together. Supervision is the key.

- Encourage group friendships between boys and girls. Discourage dating until late in the high school years. Mixed group activities are best for youth in the middle school, junior high and early high school grades.

- Electronic media dominates your child's life. Monitor their computer and cell phone use carefully. Know what sites your child visits, monitor their electronic communication and general Internet usage.

Objective

To understand the complementarity between genders

Focus

Have each student write down a career that they would like to pursue. Collect their choices and then randomly categorize the career as "Male" or "Female." Discuss the association of the genders you assigned to each career.

Explore

▸ Have students quietly read "Different and Equal."

▸ Have students identify complementary things; for example, H_2O, PB and J, the colors yellow and purple, etc. Explain: Things that are complementary complete one another. Together they produce something wonderfully new.

▸ Read the Catholics Believe box. Explain that God created both males and females for each to fulfill the needs of the other. Point out that the human race depends on the complementarity of males and females to exist.

▸ Have students read the rest of the text on the page.

Connect

▸ Return to the gender-categorized career list. Inquire: Why is it important to accept and appreciate the gender God created you to be?

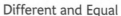

Catholics Believe

Harmony of married life and in society depends in part on the way in which the complementary needs and mutual support between the genders are lived out (CCC 2333).

Different and Equal

Maybe your mom is an "I-can-fix-anything" kind of woman, comfortable with a power drill in her hand. Perhaps your dad is the best cook you know. Is that surprising to you? Some people would view these images as surprising, even "odd." Why might that be? It is because they have a false understanding of gender and gender differences. They believe that there is a fundamental inequality between boys and girls, men and woman.

God created humans male and female, he created both equally in his image. The Gospel clearly teaches that Jesus lived this truth. He treated both men and women with "equal" respect and as having equal dignity. The Church also clearly teaches that God has given men and women equal personal dignity.

Women and men possess differences that balance and complete, or complement, each other. When they honor one another, respect one another's gifts and work together as suitable partners, they are images of the beauty and goodness of God. When women and men use these differences as a source of power to dominate one another, God and his plan of creation is dishonored and not shown respect.

 Think about the different kinds of growth and maturity that you have recently experienced.

Sexual Identity

Some people have created stereotypes of what it means to be a "man" or a "woman." A stereotype is a generalization about some group in society. It confuses individual observations with a whole group. It is easy to see how false stereotypes can result in people not respecting one another.

As individuals, each person has God-given gifts. Through personal persistent attention and appreciation of your gender, you can be proud of who God created you to be. This requires diligence about your sexual identity. This kind of diligence can be a healthy way of understanding why God

Teaching Tip

Showing Complementarity: Set up a display of complementary items that include colors, foods, themes, images, etc. Show how when complementary things interact or mix, they produce something vibrant or wonderfully new. For example, peanut butter and jelly each have a distinctive taste, yet when mixed together in sandwich form, they produce an amazing new taste. Chefs use the complementary tastes of foods to create tasty new dishes. And artists use complementary colors in creating amazing new designs that entice a person to see things in a new way.

created you male or female. God created humans with two kinds of bodies, two complementary genders, two different kinds of persons.

Complementarity is the Creator's gift to humanity. Men and women are created to live with and for each other as equals. Women and men are to help each other complete God's plan on earth. This is how men and women are unique and in need of each other to live and to love, especially in marriage.

This is part of God's plan. We exist and continue to exist based on the complementary relationship of men and women. Life and love are instrumental to our existence. When men and women share their unique gifts for the good of the family and the world, they are images, living signs, of the mystery of God's love at work in their lives and in the world.

Growing in Virtue

To accept and appreciate the gender God created you to be is a **diligent** way of understanding your sexual identity. Be proud of who you are with unique gifts, persevering as a young man or young woman according to God's plan.

"Viewing the Genders"

In the space below, outline a review of your favorite movie or show. Describe how the gender differences are treated. Equal? Complementary? Negative stereotype?

Activity

Gender 29

▶ Read the Growing in Virtue box. Explain that part of God's plan for you is to mature according to your gender.

▶ On a sheet of paper, have students anonymously complete the statement: "I'm proud to be a boy or girl because . . ." Collect the papers and read them aloud. Tell students how important it is for them to value their gender and to be proud of who they are. Point out that children who have pride in themselves are less likely to be fooled by flattery or "grooming" techniques.

▶ Explain that being diligent about one's gender helps a person find ways to appreciate their sexual identity.

▶ Use the music analogy in the reading to describe the importance of being diligent about one's gender and the complementarity of genders. The orchestra would not be able to play harmonious sounds if all the instruments made the same sound or were used contrary to their design.

▶ Have students complete the activity on the page. If needed, have them finish the activity at home with their family.

▶ Time permitting, discuss how gender stereotypes are contrary to complementarity. Use the example of sports, medicine or construction. Explain that a person's gender is never an obstacle to their contributing to the good of society.

Extending the Lesson

Using Activity Master 4A: Use the Activity Master "Your New Image." This activity helps students to monitor their feelings toward their changing self-image. Three main areas are covered: relationships, responsibilities and poise.

Debating Gender: Divide the class into groups. Assign half of each group the task of preparing arguments to defend the statement "Seventh grade boys and girls are very similar." The other half of each group is to defend the statement "Seventh grade boys and girls are very different." Be alert to the four dimensions of maturity, three aspects of gender, complementarity and gender stereotyping.

Objective

To explore attitudes about being created as male or female

Focus

Read Ephesians 5:21–33. Ask: How is love defined? Explain that St. Paul defines love in the context of marriage according to the Golden Rule and the relationship between Christ and the Church.

Discover

Read the Catholic Family Album. Ask: How did St. Paul explain the complementarity of genders in Ephesians 5? *(In the context of subordinate love; husbands and wives help each other to live holy lives.)*

Integrate

▶ Read "Part of God's Plan." Explain that our attitudes can influence our actions. Valuing who they are as boys and girls will give youth confidence to make good decisions at difficult times.

▶ Have students complete the activity on the page.

▶ Time permitting, have students list qualities they admire in another person. Then challenge them to tally or categorize those qualities as related to gender.

Pray

Invite students to write a prayer based upon their responses to the questions in this section.

Catholic Family Album

Paul of Tarsus, Apostle to the Gentiles, encountered the Risen Christ on the road to Damascus. This experience resulted in him becoming a disciple of Christ who zealously proclaimed Jesus Christ to Gentiles and, through his writings, reminded the early Church of the teachings of Christ. Many of Paul's letters are found in the New Testament and are part of the Canon of Scripture. In the Letter to the Ephesians, which is attributed to Paul, Paul described the relationship of Christ to his Church like the relationship of a husband and wife. Each must love the other with mutual respect.

Part of God's Plan

Both genders, which complement each other, are very much equal parts of God's plan for the human race. At your age, you may concentrate a bit more on the differences. But you also need to learn what human beings share in common. Neither gender is better than the other. God wants everyone to appreciate their own gender and to respect the gender of others.

Explore some of your own attitudes about what it means to be male or female. Complete the sentences that follow.

1. *My favorite toy when I was very young was*

_____

2. *A quality I most admire in someone of the other gender is*

_____

3. *What I most like about myself is*

_____

4. *A quality I hope to develop is*

_____

Reflect for a moment on the gift of your sexuality. Then make this faith choice to honor and respect your sexuality and the sexuality of others:

I will show that I appreciate the equal dignity of both genders by

_____

_____

What I will do?

30   Gender

Extending the Lesson

Using Activity Master 4B: Use the Activity Master "Expectations." This activity helps students examine their own attitudes and judgments about others. Through a series of associations the student will be challenged to match a given task to a particular kind of person.

Researching Saints: Have the students find examples of saints in the Church who promoted the complementarity between genders or rejected gender stereotypes. Such examples might include: St. Camillus of Lellis, founder of male nurses; St. Frances Xavier Cabrini, patron of hospital administrators; or Sts. Joan of Arc and Martin of Tours, patrons of soldiers.

Activity Master 4A

Name

Your New Image

As your body matures and changes, it takes time to get used to your new image. Don't panic—you'll still be you. You can handle the changes in your own particular style. Take a minute to check out your feelings.

1. Relationships

In what way do you think that relationships with your friends are getting more difficult?

_____

_____

What old rules about friendship still work?

_____

_____

2. Responsibilities

How do you feel about the new responsibilities you're taking on as you mature?

_____

_____

What strategy could you use when you're facing a responsibility you can't quite deal with?

_____

_____

3. Poise

"Poised" means feeling reasonably graceful and at home in your body. (Think how you can build on the times when you feel most comfortable with your body.)

When do you feel most poised?

_____

When do you feel least poised?

_____

Family Life Grade 7

Activity Master 4B

Name

Expectations

Do you make snap judgements about people? Cut out the figures, roll and glue them as shown so they stand up. Answer the questions. (On what are you basing your expectations?) Try the experiment on someone outside the classroom.

Which person would you choose to

help you with math?	listen to your troubles?
play drums in your band?	fix broken machinery?
teach you to cook?	help you write a poem?
go fishing with?	coach you in a new sport?
paint a poster?	teach you about baby-sitting?

Family Life Grade 7

How to Find It
How to Use It

Step 1: Click & Select

 Go to RCLBFamilyLife.com
Click on the link for activities.
Then select the activity master you need.

Step 2: Print & Copy

 Print each activity master in advance.
Then copy enough for everyone in the class.

Step 3: Share & Discuss

 Once students have completed the activity,
have them share and discuss their responses.

REVIEWING UNIT 2

Summary

► Ask the students to read through the Summary section.

► Invite them to ask questions about any points that are not clear to them.

► Make sure to expand on any points that were perhaps touched on only lightly during class time.

Thinking It Through

► Have students answer all three questions on the page.

► Assign each student a number from one through three.

► Have students share with the class their answer to the question that corresponds to their assigned number.

Matching It Up

Use this matching section to help the students identify the appropriate definition or description of a key concept, term or person from the unit.

Name ....

Summary

Remember what you have learned in each of the lessons in God's Gift of Self.

LESSON 3: Identity

• During adolescence you are maturing physically, mentally, emotionally and spiritually.

• Spiritual maturity is a lifelong growth process that focuses on living as Christ did.

• God created you—all of you. Much searching for self-identity occurs during adolescence.

LESSON 4: Gender

• God created the human race with two genders. Gender is a person's sexual identity as a male or female.

• The differences between men and women are not signs of their inequality. The way these differences work together is called complementarity.

• God desires for you to accept and appreciate the gender he created you to be.

Thinking It Through

1. How have you grown spiritually in the last year?

....

....

....

2. How do students in your school show respect toward people of the other gender?

....

....

....

3. Identify one masculine and one feminine image that would help you personalize your relationship with God?

....

....

....

....

Matching It Up

On each line, write the letter of the description in Column B that best goes with the term in Column A.

A		**B**
1. **D** Adolescence		**A.** The ability to adjust to change or capacity to recover from change
2. **C** Complementarity		**B.** Personal persistent attention and appreciation for who you are and what you do
3. **B** Diligence		**C.** To live with and for each other as equal in dignity and unique in gender to complete God's plan
4. **E** Maturity		**D.** A stage of life between childhood and adulthood
5. **A** Resilience		**E.** The process whereby one realizes their full potential

REVIEWING UNIT 2

Name ....

Recalling Key Concepts

Circle the T if the statement is true. Circle the F if the statement is false.

1. Normally the ability to think abstractly will decrease during adolescence.   T   **(F)**
2. God created human beings different in gender and therefore unequal in dignity.   T   **(F)**
3. Growing in Christian maturity is a lifelong process.   **(T)**   F
4. Males and females are different in opposite ways.   T   **(F)**
5. A person's physical growth is determined by the reproductive system.   T   **(F)**

Fill in the missing words in these sentences.

6. ....**GENDER**.... refers to a person's sexual identity as male or female.

7. By following ....**JESUS**.... and the way he lived, you can be a positive role model for others.

8. ....**HORMONES**.... are chemicals that act as messengers throughout the body setting things in motion for the body to grow and mature.

9. When you ....**STEREOTYPE**.... others, you erroneously generalize and expect all people in a certain role to act or be the same.

10. The three aspects of a person's gender include: physical, ...**PSYCHOLOGICAL**.... and spiritual.

Working Together

In a group, look through fashion advertisements. Each person in the group should pick one image and evaluate it on how it respects and honors the person and his or her gender. Discuss how these images influence you in helping or hindering your ability to accept and appreciate the gender God created you to be.

32   Unit 2 Review

Recalling Key Concepts

► Use this section to help the students be able to accurately recall the key concepts from the unit.

► For the true and false section, you can have students correct any false statements.

► To help with the fill-in section, you might want to provide a word bank on the board.

Working Together

► Choose a project that best fits the need and abilities of your students, as well as your time schedule.

► Time permitting, have students complete the unit assessment individually or as a class; otherwise encourage them to complete it at home.

Teaching Tip

Metaphors: Ask students to create their own metaphor for God to help them develop a closer relationship with him. Have them begin with the words: "God is like . . ."
Point out that metaphors could describe inanimate objects, such as a shield (Psalm 84:12) and animals or other living creatures (Hosea 5:14). Ask them to work in small groups and to share their work with the whole class once completed.

UNIT 3
God's Gift of Life

Background

"For by His incarnation the Son of God has united Himself in some fashion with every man. He worked with human hands, He thought with a human mind, acted by human choice and loved with a human heart. Born of the Virgin Mary, He has truly been made one of us, like us in all things except sin" (Gaudium et Spes *22*).

IN GOD'S PLAN OF CREATION, THE BEAUTY AND goodness of all Creation is revealed in humankind, the high point of the divine plan. And at the center of the divine plan of Salvation, of the New Creation, is Jesus Christ, the incarnate Son of God, human like us in all things but sin. "And the Word became flesh / and made his dwelling among us" (John 1:14). Joined to Christ through Baptism, we are part of this new creation. Saint Paul reminds us "Whoever is in Christ is a new creation" (2 Corinthians 5:17). We are also called to maturity as persons, just as Jesus grew in age and wisdom in his life at Nazareth with Mary and Joseph. Respecting ourselves as persons created in the image of God and created anew in Christ begins in the Christian family.

GOD ENTRUSTS OUR LIFE TO US. WE ARE TO BE GOOD stewards of the gift of our life and the life of others. The care we show for our life and the life of others manifests respect for oneself and for others as God's good creation. The media often tries to sell beauty and the care of one's body as the number one priority. Adolescents are susceptible to such advertisements. We need to help them approach advertising critically. They need to see that goodness and beauty cannot be bought and sold. They need to value themselves

as created good and beautiful, and understand that their task is to value and take care of themselves—their mind, body and spirit.

Good health is not simply an absence of physical sickness or pain. It is a state of the well-being of the whole person—mind, body and spirit. Just as the body needs care and nourishment, the spiritual side of the human person also needs care and nourishment. All people—children, young people and adults—have the responsibility to care for both their physical and spiritual health.

SUBSTANCE ABUSE IN OUR SOCIETY IS WIDESPREAD. For some young people, substance abuse is not a theoretical dilemma. Some know from experience that drug and alcohol abuse has costly and tragic effects on individuals, families and society. Substance abuse damages relationships and it interferes with God's mission for individuals. The abuse of drugs inflicts damage not only on human health but also on human life.

If young people are well-informed about the dangers of using drugs, alcohol and tobacco and are secure about their identity and dignity, they are in a strong

> ### Additional Background
>
> *Catechism of the Catholic Church:* §§ 1706, 2258–2283, 2319, 2322, 2348–2350

position to make good and healthy choices. While the number of abusers is large and the consequences are frightening, the number of those who do not take drugs is even larger. Adolescents need to hear this positive and hope-filled message. As a teacher you have the opportunity to present clear, vital information. This can help your students to make the choices that promote their health—physical, emotional and spiritual.

For Reflection

Read and reflect on the following:

"Life and physical heath are precious gifts entrusted to us by God. We must take reasonable care of them, taking into account the needs of others and the common good" (Catechism of the Catholic Church *2288*).

▶ How would I rate the plan I have for caring for my physical well-being? My spiritual well-being? What improvements might I make?

▶ What might we do as a class to design and implement a "Wellness Plan"?

Child Safety

Young teens, stuck in the throes of puberty, often feel unattractive, unwanted and unloved. This may leave them vulnerable to anyone who is kind to them or who pays them any positive attention. These lessons will help the students to feel better about and take better care of themselves and provide support to faltering egos and battered self-esteem. Strong self-confidence is one of the greatest defenses against those who seek to take advantage of young people.

Family Time

Partnering with the Family

Respecting ourselves as persons of immense value begins in the family. So too does the process of accepting all of our distinctiveness. Accepting daughters and sons as each has been created is part of the work of parents. Encourage the parents of your students to review the materials covered in this unit with their child. Make available and suggest that families use the Parent Connection in addition to the Family Time pages to discuss the topics of wellness and the gift of life. Families do well to give thanks for all God's gifts, especially the gift of children.

Goal: To discover the beauty of the body and how good health habits give glory to God, the source of all beauty

Engage
Page 65

Objective
To understand God as the source of goodness and beauty

Family Time
Ensure that each student tears out their Family Time page to complete at home.

Pray
Psalm 27:4–10

Focus
Judge a beauty contest.

Discover
Discuss the connection between beauty and good health.

Teach
Page 66

Objective
To identify how a person can care for their own personal hygiene

Focus
Decorate a drawing of a body with health-care advertisements.

Explore
Read, discuss and summarize the importance of personal hygiene and the differences between good and bad health habits.
Catholics Believe: The human body reflects divine beauty.

Connect
Growing in Virtue: Being responsible for wellness
Describe the influence and impact of trends on body image.

Apply
Page 68

Objective
To evaluate personal health habits and wellness practices

Focus
Discuss what it takes to care for items from daily life.

Discover
Catholic Family Album: Catholic hospitals

Integrate
Complete a personal health checklist for wellness

Pray
Reflect on God as the source of beauty.

Vocabulary Preview

Hygiene—practice of cleanliness that promotes good health

Nutrition—the study of foods and how the human body uses them

Perspiration—the production and excretion of moisture from the sweat glands; increases during stress, cools the body

Wellness—soundness of mind, body and spirit; same as healthy living

Materials Needed

▶ writing paper
▶ pens, pencils
▶ art supplies
▶ health-care product advertisements
▶ Bible
▶ Lesson 5 Activity Masters

Call to Prayer
Jesus, you saw, respected and enjoyed the natural beauty of creation. Teach me to appreciate the beauty in our world, especially in myself and in others. Help me to guide my students toward a healthy body image. Amen.

Wellness

God's Beautiful Creation

Wildflowers are a lesson in beauty, living signs that manifest the Beauty of God. Wildflowers grow everywhere: in woods, fields, deserts, jungles and swamps. All shapes and sizes grow side by side.

Wildflowers can remind us of people. People are beautiful just as they come, in all colors and shapes. God's creation is filled with infinite variety and beauty. People are God's greatest creation. They are images of God, of the Beauty and Goodness of God.

Sometimes this fundamental beauty of a person is disregarded because a person may not "measure up" to society's standards. For example, the beauty of a heavy person may not be seen when the trend and standard of society is "Thin is in." A short person may not look "beautiful" to a person who thinks beauty is in height. The fundamental, God-given beauty and goodness of each and every person cannot be measured by the ever-changing standards of a society.

People in Bloom

A flower has several stages of growth, from foliage to bud to blooming plant. The beauty and goodness of a plant or flower is sometimes not seen in the "bud." But it is there. You are experiencing a similar type of growth. You might think of it as your "budding" stage. Your mind and body are moving toward full development. All that you will be is not yet visible.

During this stage, you can do a lot to look and feel truly good. You can take good care of your body inside and out. Taking care of you on the "inside" can pay off on the "outside." When you eat healthful foods, exercise regularly and respect yourself and others, you're making a statement. You are saying, "God made me very good" (based on Genesis 1:31).

> **This lesson will help you to:**
> - **explore** that God is the source of goodness and beauty.
> - **understand** the importance of taking greater personal responsibility for your hygiene.
> - **evaluate** your own personal wellness.

 What are your standards of beauty? Do they help or keep you from seeing the beauty and goodness of others?

Wellness **35**

Teaching Tip

To Behold Beauty: Reflect on the Old English word *behold*. It means "to keep hold of, to view, to look at." Given the amount of visual stimulation that people experience today in the mass media and online, help your students pause or slow down when viewing images and things during this lesson so that they can "keep hold" or behold the beauty present. Evaluate how the classroom is set up to determine if students are able to behold the beauty of the various things and images on display. Consider how artwork is framed; find a way to better display the image so a person can behold its beauty. Or imagine the space of a museum, each object should be given a specific amount of space to aid viewers in beholding that which is before them.

ENGAGE

Objective
To understand God as the source of goodness and beauty

Pray
Open the lesson by reading Psalm 27:4–10. Then reflect on the desire to see God's beauty.

Focus
Have students judge a beauty contest using three images: nature, a church and a baby. They are to rate them from most beautiful to least. Discuss the students' criteria, their idea of beauty and the source of their perception.

Discover
▶ Read "God's Beautiful Creation." Inquire: How is beauty not in the eye of the beholder? Then read the rest of the text.

▶ Explain that if God, Creator of all, is the source of beauty, then beauty can be found in everything and everyone. This beauty can never be lost, but it can be hidden by sin.

▶ Discuss how beauty and good health are related. Explain that good health includes one's physical, mental, emotional and spiritual health.

▶ Form groups of four. Have groups make a list of qualities needed for physical, mental, emotional and spiritual beauty. Discuss the reasons students included each of the qualities they chose.

TEACH

To identify how a person can care for their own personal hygiene

Focus

Draw a body outline on the board and have students "decorate" the body with health-care advertisements. Discuss how these ads might promote either good or bad health habits.

Explore

▶ Have students identify people who model good health habits and discuss how their influence has helped them.

▶ Have students quietly read "Personal Hygiene."

▶ Have students make a list of people whom they trust and in whom they can confide.

▶ Using the body drawing, have students replace those ads that promote bad habits with ones that promote good health; for example, weight-loss pills might be replaced with a nutritional diet.

▶ Read Catholics Believe. Explain that God created the human body to reflect divine beauty. Caring for our bodies is a way of honoring God for this great gift.

▶ Discuss what healthy habits can still be added to the body drawing.

Catholics Believe

Life and physical health are precious gifts entrusted to us by God, the Author of life and beauty. The human body is a temple of the Holy Spirit. It is a manifestation of divine beauty (CCC 2288, 2519).

Personal Hygiene

Taking care of yourself includes making choices that promote your wellness. For much of your basic physical wellness, you depend on doctors and nurses and other health-care professionals. Regular examinations ensure that you are healthy both physically and psychologically. They can help prevent illness or discover disease early enough for you to receive proper care.

Through personal hygiene, you can be responsible for and can contribute to your wellness, your sense of health and well-being. The good habit of daily personal hygiene helps to promote your good health and wellness.

 Think about the various ways in which you take care of yourself in mind, body and spirit.

Basic health care begins with soap and water. Daily bathing, shampooing and the cleaning and clipping of fingernails all contribute to the practice of wellness. Teenagers experience an increase in perspiration. When perspiration mixes with bacteria, it can result in an unpleasant body order. Washing daily and using deodorant will help you be, feel and smell clean. Good health care also includes exercising daily and wearing clean, sensible, modest and comfortable clothing. Do not forget that you also need a good night's sleep.

Good body care includes the care of your teeth and eyes. Your teeth need brushing after meals, flossing and regular checkups with a dentist. You also need to take care of your eyesight by having regular vision checks. If you have glasses or wear contact lenses, take care of them. Always wear proper eye protection whenever necessary, like when you are playing sports.

Nutrition is also a vital part of wellness. You are growing fast and need plenty of healthful foods. Be attentive to the types and amounts of food you choose to eat. Eat a balanced diet that includes foods that promote good health, such as breads and grains, fruits and vegetables, meat and fish and low-fat milk products. Adolescence is the time when most eating disorders, such as anorexia and bulimia, start.

36 Wellness

Teaching Tip

Body Decoration: Spend some time discussing the issue related to body decorating, such as body piercing, branding, tattooing, hair dying and the general use of cosmetics. The discussion of these issues will depend on the students' familiarity with each type of body decoration. The Church neither explicitly prohibits body decorations nor promotes the practice. However, mutilating the body can be morally wrong and a sign of emotional need. Many cultures view body decorations as a sign of prestige and a way to honor the human body.

People suffering from these and other eating disorders need immediate medical and psychological help. While you need to be conscious of your weight, realize that your weight, like the rest of your physical growth, will vary and change. Watch and care for it wisely.

Wellness also includes caring for your mind and spirit. Since your primary focus is on school, you will need to balance your time between study, recreation and relaxation. Give attention to all aspects of your growth: physical, mental, emotional and spiritual. With all the busy activities going on in your life, choose time each and every day to develop your relationship with God. Set aside time to be alone with God in prayer. Take part regularly in Mass with your family and parish community. Decide for yourself to take part with your friends in the life of your parish.

Growing in Virtue

The **Fifth Commandment** teaches that your are to be responsible for your safety and wellness, for the gift of your life. You have the responsibility to attend to your physical, mental, emotional and spiritual well-being. The good decisions you make can result in feeling and being healthy and holy.

"The Empty Well"

Identify a current fad or trend that does not promote your physical or spiritual wellness. Write it on the outside of the well. On the inside of the well, write why it might make a person feel empty inside.

Activity

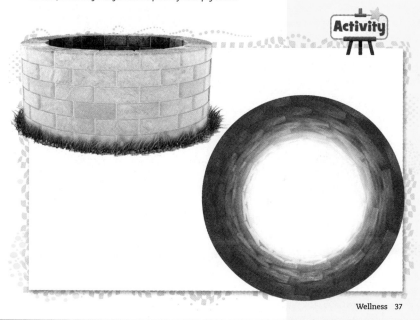

Extending the Lesson

Using Activity Master 5A: Use the Activity Master "What's Beautiful." This activity will help students examine and evaluate societal standards about beauty through designing an advertisement about a "beauty" product.

Human Figure in Art: Collect age-appropriate images that reflect the diversity of beauty across cultures today and in the past. Statues or portraits can be helpful guides as to what a particular culture considers "beautiful." Just a few examples from art history include the *Venus of Villendorf*, Ancient Egyptian figures in relief, statues from Greek and Roman Antiquity, paintings by Botticelli, Titian and Manet, as well as the human figure depicted by Picasso or Matisse.

Connect

▶ Read the Growing in Virtue box. Have students identify how certain bad health habits dealing with the body can impact the non-physical health aspects of a person.

▶ Ask students what they think "self-confidence" means. Caution that high confidence can lead to pride while low self-image can lead to despair. Have students identify what makes them feel good about themselves and what makes them feel less confident.

▶ Explain that people with healthy self-esteem do not need others to always tell them how good they are and so are not as susceptible to sexual grooming. Review the concept of sexual grooming.

▶ Explain that responsibly caring for ourselves takes effort, but that effort pays off in self-confidence especially in our abilities.

▶ Have students complete the activity on the page. If needed, have them finish the activity at home with their family.

▶ Discuss the difference between self-confidence and a false sense of pride. How can too much confidence be harmful? *(You might take unreasonable risks.)* How can too much focus on looking or feeling good be detrimental? *(Over-exercising or over-eating or primping in the mirror constantly can be signs of low self-image.)*

Objective

To evaluate personal health habits and wellness practices

Focus

Have students make a list of items from daily life that require maintenance and care.

Discover

Read the Catholic Family Album. Ask: How does the Catholic Church support wellness? *(Part of her mission is to care for those who are sick; therefore, the Church has many hospitals.)*

Integrate

▶ Read "Making Wellness Decisions." Have students add a "support network" to the list. Why is a support network important for health? Have students make a list of all of the people who are a part of their support networks—people they can turn to when needed.

▶ Have students complete the activity on the page.

▶ Time permitting, collect tallies from students on those line items they are doing well and discuss potential reasons for their success.

Pray

Invite students to reflect on the saying by St. Augustine "The beauty of creation bears witness to God." Then have them prayerfully read one of the following Scripture passages: Psalm 8 and 19, Ecclesiastes 3 or Revelation 4.

Catholic Family Album

Catholic hospitals are dedicated to the well-being of people. Today, in the United States there are more than 950 hospitals and other health-care facilities serving more than seven million people. While hospitals, as we know them today, were not established until much later, they have their origins in the ministry of the early Church. During the second through fifth centuries this ministry was considered primarily the work of the deacons. **Saint John of God** (1495–1550), founder of the Brothers Hospitallers, is the patron saint of hospitals and hospital workers.

Making Wellness Decisions

Do a quick personal wellness check-up. Read and think about each statement on the chart at the bottom of this page. Put a "W" if you think you are doing well. Mark an "I" if you think you need improvement. When you are finished, choose one or two of the items you marked "I" and write a short plan that shows how you will take greater responsibility for your wellness.

1. *General Hygiene*
   __ Get adequate sleep every night
   __ Take a bath or shower every day
   __ Shampoo frequently
   __ Keep nails clean and trimmed
   __ Use deodorant
   __ Wear clean clothes

2. *Dental and Eye Care*
   __ Brush teeth after meals
   __ Floss regularly
   __ Avoid sugary foods and drinks
   __ See a dentist twice a year
   __ See an eye doctor regularly
   __ Use good lighting
   __ Protect your eyes

3. *Nutrition*
   __ Eat breakfast every day
   __ Portion food appropriate to body type
   __ Eat fresh fruits and vegetables daily
   __ Drink eight glasses of water a day
   __ Follow the food pyramid
   __ Exercise every day

4. *Care of Mind and Spirit*
   __ Spend time doing recreational activities
   __ Read for fun and enrichment
   __ Devote time for reflection in silence
   __ Participate in parish life
   __ Pray every day

38   Wellness

Extending the Lesson

Using Activity Master 5B: Use the Activity Master "Grooming Crossword." This crossword puzzle activity will help students identify key terms relevant to good health habits for personal hygiene.

Guest Speaker: Invite a health-care professional to talk with the students about the importance of personal hygiene. Encourage students to ask questions, but allow the speaker to offer solid information. Be sure to inform parents in advance about the guest speaker and invite the parents to be present. Note that while the youth are responsible for their own good health habits, the family can be supportive of their efforts.

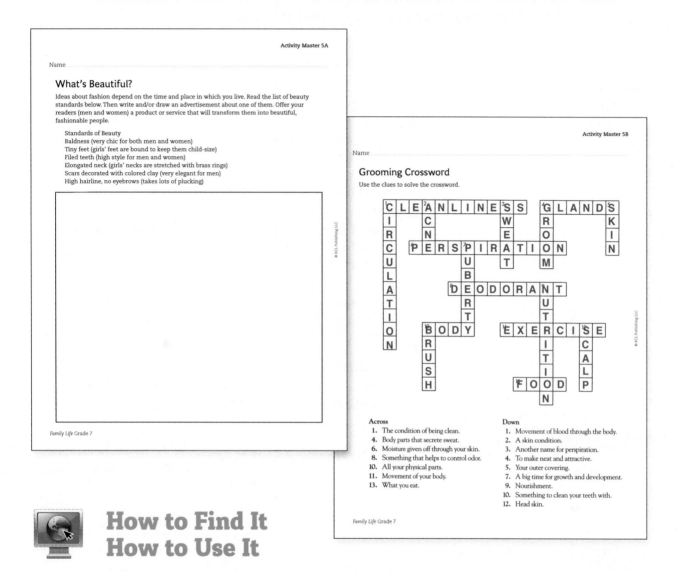

Activity Master 5A

Name ....

What's Beautiful?

Ideas about fashion depend on the time and place in which you live. Read the list of beauty standards below. Then write and/or draw an advertisement about one of them. Offer your readers (men and women) a product or service that will transform them into beautiful, fashionable people.

Standards of Beauty
Baldness (very chic for both men and women)
Tiny feet (girls' feet are bound to keep them child-size)
Filed teeth (high style for men and women)
Elongated neck (girls' necks are stretched with brass rings)
Scars decorated with colored clay (very elegant for men)
High hairline, no eyebrows (takes lots of plucking)

Family Life Grade 7

Activity Master 5B

Name ....

Grooming Crossword

Use the clues to solve the crossword.

Across
1. The condition of being clean.
4. Body parts that secrete sweat.
6. Moisture given off through your skin.
8. Something that helps to control odor.
10. All your physical parts.
11. Movement of your body.
13. What you eat.

Down
1. Movement of blood through the body.
2. A skin condition.
3. Another name for perspiration.
4. To make neat and attractive.
5. Your outer covering.
7. A big time for growth and development.
9. Nourishment.
10. Something to clean your teeth with.
12. Head skin.

Family Life Grade 7

How to Find It
How to Use It

Step 1: Click & Select

Go to RCLBFamilyLife.com
Click on the link for activities.
Then select the activity master you need.

Step 2: Print & Copy

Print each activity master in advance.
Then copy enough for everyone in the class.

Step 3: Share & Discuss

Once students have completed the activity,
have them share and discuss their responses.

Goal: To evaluate the choices we have in dealing with addictive substances through accurate information and spiritual guidance

Engage
Page 71

Objective
To understand that life choices are part of growing up

Pray
Seek guidance on choosing the gift of life.

Focus
Identify age-appropriate choices.

Discover
Facilitate a discussion on why people use addictive substances.

Teach
Page 72

Objective
To identify the kinds of addictive substances and the risks of each

Focus
Assess students' prior knowledge of the effects of drug abuse.

Explore
Read, discuss and summarize the impact and effects of various kinds of addictive substances, legal and illegal.
Catholics Believe: Human life must be respected.

Connect
Growing in Virtue: Choosing to say yes to good health habits
Write a commercial script and evaluate its effectiveness.

Apply
Page 73

Objective
To use faith as a source of strength in resisting temptation

Focus
Luke 22:39–46

Discover
Catholic Family Album: Catholic Charities USA

Integrate
Pledge in prayer seeking spiritual strength to resist temptation.

Pray
The Lord's Prayer, especially "Lead us not into temptation"

Reviewing Unit 3
Summarize and review the content from both lessons.

Vocabulary Preview

Addiction—the mental or physical craving for or dependence on a substance

Cirrhosis—a disease of the liver that prevents it from removing harmful substances from the blood

Intoxication—coming from the Latin word meaning "poisoned," the diminishing effects on the physical or mental abilities to function normally

Temptation—an attraction either from outside oneself or from within to act contrary to right reason and the Commandments of God

Materials Needed

- writing paper
- pens, pencils
- art supplies
- Bible
- Lesson 6 Activity Masters

Call to Prayer

Lord, give each of us, especially young people today, the courage and strength to resist every form of temptation. Let all of us find meaning and joy in life and provide us the clear virtuous path of prudence and patience. Amen.

Choose Life

The World of Drugs

The Swine Flu pandemic began to spread throughout the world in 2009. Researchers began studying the H1N1 virus closely and developed a vaccine to protect people. Scientists, chemists and other researchers have and continue to discover the wonder of God's creation and to use those discoveries to help the human family.

Among those discoveries are "drugs." A drug is any chemical or combination of chemicals that can be used to interact with the body's chemistry. Drugs are meant to help the body fight disease or to provide protection. Some drugs are legal and available by prescription only; others are easily available over the counter. When used correctly, these drugs can contribute to our well-being.

This lesson will help you to:

- **explore** that life choices are a part of growing up.
- **discover** and understand some dangers of substance abuse.
- **use** your faith to help resist temptation to misuse or abuse drugs.

Living Dangerously

There is another side, a dark side, to the world of drugs. Just because a substance is legal does not mean it cannot be abused. A person can choose to use drugs illegally and in a way that harms the body. This is called drug abuse or substance abuse.

Despite many warnings and sad stories of people, including family and friends, some people abuse drugs even to the point of dying from them. Research shows that teenagers misuse and abuse drugs and other chemical substances because (1) they see others do it, (2) it helps them feel a certain way that they would not feel without the drug and (3) they think that it can solve a problem. People who abuse drugs live dangerously. First, substance abuse can easily lead to drug addiction. Second, this kind of addiction often leads to a slow death.

 What evidence have you seen that substance abuse is a problem for young people?

Choose Life 39

Teaching Tip

Why People Use: Because of the science and studies on addictive substances and their abuse, you might want to invite a trained professional to speak on the effects of addictive substances. A trained professional could help expand the lesson more on why people use them. Then, after hearing the guest speaker, you can guide a conversation into a discussion of alternative choices to drug abuse and of supporting mechanisms that could prevent substance abuse or help someone who is struggling through their addiction. Research shows that presenting only negative outcomes does not discourage negative behavior. The key is to offer other, positive alternatives.

ENGAGE

Objective

To understand that life choices are part of growing up

Pray

Open the lesson with a prayer seeking guidance from the Lord on discerning the best ways to choose life right now.

Focus

On a three-column chart, have volunteers write specific life choices made by a child of seven, a seventh grader and a senior in high school. Discuss the importance of choices according to age and maturity.

Discover

▶ Read the text on the page. Clarify the proper use of drugs versus their abuse.

▶ Inquire: What pressures do young people face today regarding substance abuse? What are some of the ways that they cope with those pressures?

▶ Stress the value of having a strong support network of adults whom you can turn to when you have problems, even embarrassing ones.

▶ Facilitate a conversation on some of the positive and negative peer pressures related to substance abuse.

Objective

To identify the kinds of addictive substances and the risks of each

Focus

Assess your students' level of factual knowledge about addictive substances by asking them to tell how the body is affected by nicotine, alcohol and illegal drugs. This will help you in guiding them through this lesson.

Explore

▶ Have students quietly read "Choosing Not To." Then, as a class read the text aloud; pause for students to react or ask questions.

▶ Explain that society permits the regulated and moderate use of tobacco and alcohol. And the Church does not prohibit the moderate use of these substances either.

▶ Inquire: Why do you think people choose to use drugs or alcohol? Point out that many teens drink, smoke or take illegal drugs because they want to "act like an adult" or want to escape from issues they find too difficult to handle. Both of these reasons show a low self-image. Students with self-confidence, who value who they are, like their bodies and who love their lives are less likely to use or abuse tobacco, alcohol or illegal drugs.

▶ Have students brainstorm a list of things they can do to feel good without using alcohol or drugs.

Catholics Believe

Human life must be respected; behaviors that destroy or seriously damage human life or health are a grave offense against the Fifth Commandment. Production of and trafficking in drugs are acts gravely contrary to the moral law.

Choosing Not To

Much of the substance abuse today involves three types of substances: nicotine products, alcoholic beverages and illegal drugs. It is much easier to choose not to have anything to do with these substances than it is to stop using them after you are addicted. It is important to understand about the addictive qualities of drugs and other chemical substances. This knowledge can help you to use prescription and over-the-counter drugs appropriately and to resist the temptation of using illegal drugs.

Remember that drugs produce only a short-term "good" effect when used appropriately. When their use is abused, they create the long-term effect of dependency, an addiction. Because of the physical interaction between these addictive substances and the body of the user, the chemical reaction among persons varies. The result is that some people more easily become dependent on or addicted to the use of a particular substance. This means that a person may have less control than others in the ability to reject or resist the temptation to use an addictive substance. For all of us, the excessive use of anything is unhealthy and can be dangerous. Let's take a look at two of the most common drugs and substances whose use often leads to abuse, dependency and addiction.

 Think about some of the temptations you are facing in your life now.

Tobacco contains a highly addictive substance called *nicotine*. Within eight seconds of being inhaled, nicotine reaches the brain. Many of the other chemicals in tobacco products are poisonous and may eventually lead to cancer or lung disease. Smokers who begin using nicotine before age fifteen have a cancer rate nineteen times higher than people who begin smoking later in life. Every nicotine product carries the same or similar risks.

Alcohol is found in beer, wine and liquor. Every producer of alcoholic beverages is required by law to identify how much alcohol is contained in their products. This is called the proof number. Alcohol begins to affect the body immediately. Because alcohol flows to all parts of the body through the

40   Choose Life

Teaching Tip

Self-Evaluation: Complete a self-evaluation using the questions provided here, then have the students complete the evaluation. Inform the students that you also completed the evaluation and this is a personal and private exercise. The point of the exercise is to give them time for reflection so they can better evaluate how they have been acting and so they can improve their good health habits. (1) Do I see in myself or others drinking or eating in response to problems? (2) Do I see in others or myself performance or grades beginning to fall? (3) Do I see in others or myself using a daily "pick-me-up" habit, like in caffeinated drinks? (4) Do I find myself resistant or easily agitated by others? Remind the students that addictive substances bring only short-term effects, leaving the individual's health damaged.

blood stream, every body system is at risk. Alcohol impairs a person, making it difficult to function and make decisions. It changes a person's perception, impairing a person's ability to drive and even walk. Alcohol can interfere with the liver's ability to break down fats. The destruction of the liver is called *cirrhosis*. Cirrhosis is often the result of long-term abusive alcoholic drinking and is the cause of death in many people.

There are also many addictive substances that are illegal to use. Their use not only brings destruction to lives of abusers but also to their families and friends. Again you can choose to say no before you even try these drugs and avoid the risks—and slavery they bring—all together.

Growing in Virtue

Knowing the dangerous effects of addictive substances and choosing to say no is saying yes to being healthy. The virtues of **prudence** and **temperance** guide us to use drugs in the appropriate manner that benefits our well-being.

"Drugs Do Damage"

Write a script for a public service video announcement about this lesson. Have your friends evaluate how effective it is in deterring the use of addictive substances. Write the outline in the space below.

Choose Life 41

▶ Read the Catholics Believe box on the previous page. Explain that the Church permits the research and use of drugs only if such acts seek to promote life and are moral, and the research never damages or destroys human life.

▶ Place students in small groups to respond to the question: How should a person act toward someone who uses illegal drugs?

Connect

▶ Read the Growing in Virtue box. Arrange students in small groups and have them create scenarios demonstrating youth saying no to addictive drugs.

▶ Have students complete the activity on the page. If needed, have them finish the activity at home with their family.

▶ Time permitting, allow students to share their evaluation on the influence and effectiveness of ads that deter the use of drugs.

Extending the Lesson

Using Activity Master 6A: Use the Activity Master "Alternatives." This activity provides students an opportunity to further evaluate the reasons people use and abuse addictive substances. This will equip them with alternative solutions to combat the temptations involved.

Trivia Pursuit: Have students research the short-term and long-term effects of a specific addictive drug. Have them develop questions and answers to "quiz" their classmates. Be sure that they focus on the chemical effects on the body as well as the social effects on the family, friends and others. The point of this research is for the youth to become more knowledgeable about addictive substances in order to resist and to help others who may be using or attempted to use addictive substances.

Objective

To use faith as a source of strength in resisting temptation

Focus

Read Luke 22:39–46. Discuss whether the disciple gave in to temptation. Explain that Jesus models for us the watchful way of resisting temptation through understanding and prayer.

Discover

Read the Catholic Family Album. Inquire: How can you support those recovering from addiction? *(Student can at least pray for them.)*

Integrate

▶ Read "Spread the Word." Review a list of common temptations that the students are facing today. Tell them this list is for the class to pray over, asking God to give us strength in resisting them.

▶ Have students complete the activity on the page. Explain that a pledge reminds a person to be strong in will.

▶ Time permitting, share experiences when God's healing mercy enabled someone's recovery.

Pray

Invite students to pray the Lord's Prayer giving emphasis to the petition "Lead us not into temptation."

Catholic Family Album

Catholic Charities USA gives witness to the Catholic Social Teaching that every person has a basic right to adequate health care. Catholic Charities USA provides behavioral health services, which includes substance abuse treatment, to individuals and families. The importance of these services is highlighted by the fact that substance abuse affects about 22 million persons in the United States each year. Of these 22 million people, only about 3 million receive treatment. Saint Maximillian Kolbe (1894–1941) is the patron saint of drug abusers. Saint Martin of Tours (316–397) is the patron saint of alcohol abusers.

Catholic Charities USA.

Spread the Word

Substance abuse would not be a temptation if there were nothing appealing about it. Some people use addictive substances because they want to "fit in" or "feel good." Those are all temptations, or tests. Temptation is an attraction to something evil or bad for you. However, you now know that the good feeling does not last, but the bondage, or slavery to the drug, could be permanent, and even deadly.

It is a moral choice not to become involved in self-destructive behaviors, such as smoking, drinking and drug abuse. People already addicted to these behaviors need compassionate and prayerful support to transform their lives. Recovery from any addiction—and getting well again—is possible. Support groups, such as Al-Anon and Alateen, provide support for the spouse and children of the alcoholic.

A strong faith and moral foundation can help you overcome the temptation to abuse drugs and help you support someone recovering from drug abuse. In the space below, write a pledge prayer in which you ask God for strength and guidance to say no to drugs. Share your prayer with your friends and family.

My Pledge in Prayer

42   Choose Life

Extending the Lesson

Using Activity Master 6B: Use the Activity Master "What You Do to Your Body." This activity provides scientific illustrations and information about the physiological impact of both nicotine and alcohol. You might consider using this reproducible handout in conjunction with the readings in this lesson.

Road to Recovery: Inform students that the resilience of the body makes it possible to find freedom from addiction. We can also turn to others, such as support groups that provide support for everyone involved, including family members of substance abusers. The grace of God is also available to abusers in the sacraments.

Activity Master 6A

Name

Alternatives

Read the reasons people give for using drugs, and the truth behind each statement. Then find some alternatives to drug use.

"Everybody does it."
(Most people don't)

"I'm bored."
(Being in a stupor is *really* boring.)

"I need to get away from stress and pressure."
(Drug use leads to *major* stress.)

"I just want to try it once, to see what it's like."
(That's what every addict said, the first time.)

"My parents are always telling me what to do."
(When drugs take over, they control *everything* you do.)

"It makes me feel good."
(The good feelings are temporary. Later, you feel worse than ever.)

"I do better at sports." "I'm more creative." "I feel less shy."
(Drugs make you *think* you're performing well. Actually, both your brain and body are impaired.)

Write some alternatives for:

Relaxing, coping with stress

_____

_____

Conquering boredom

_____

_____

Feeling good about yourself

_____

_____

Family Life Grade 7

© RCL Publishing LLC

Activity Master 6B

Name

What You Do to Your Body . . .

When You Smoke Cigarettes.

Mouth. Your sense of taste is impaired. Your teeth are stained by tar. Smoking causes mouth and throat cancer.

Lungs. Along with nicotine, you inhale carbon monoxide, a poisonous gas. Tar coats the whole respiratory tract and destroys the surface of the lungs.

Fingers. Cigarettes cause yellow stains on fingers.

Heart and Circulatory System. Your heart speeds up and your blood pressure rises.

Digestive System. The chemicals in tobacco keep your body from making good use of proteins, carbohydrates, fats, and vitamins B and C.

Bladder, Kidney, Pancreas. You have a greater risk of developing cancer of these organs than nonsmokers.

When You Drink Alcohol.

Brain. The moment you take a drink, your circulatory system carries it to your brain, impairing your judgment and eventually damaging your brain. One ounce of alcohol can destroy one million brain cells.

Digestive System. Alcohol damages the cells of the mouth, throat, stomach, and pancreas, leading to cancer, ulcers, and gastritis.

Circulatory System. Because of its anesthetic effect on your heart, alcohol impairs your circulation. Heavy drinking causes permanent damage to the heart.

Lungs. When you inhale them, alcohol fumes are absorbed into the lungs and then pass quickly to the brain.

Liver. It takes your liver many hours to get rid of the alcohol you consume. Heavy drinking destroys liver tissue.

Family Life Grade 7

© RCL Publishing LLC

How to Find It
How to Use It

Step 1: Click & Select

Go to RCLBFamilyLife.com
Click on the link for activities.
Then select the activity master you need.

Step 2: Print & Copy

Print each activity master in advance.
Then copy enough for everyone in the class.

Step 3: Share & Discuss

Once students have completed the activity,
have them share and discuss their responses.

Summary

▶ Ask the students to read through the Summary section.

▶ Invite them to ask questions about any points that are not clear to them.

▶ Make sure to expand on any points that were perhaps touched on only lightly during class time.

Thinking It Through

▶ Have students answer all three questions on the page.

▶ Assign each student a number from one through three.

▶ Have students share with the class their answer to the question that corresponds to their assigned number.

Matching It Up

Use this matching section to help the students identify the appropriate definition or description of a key concept, term or person from the unit.

REVIEWING UNIT 3

Name ....

Summary

Remember what you have learned in each of the lessons in God's Gift of Life.

LESSON 5: Wellness

• God is the source of beauty, and your body reflects divine beauty.

• Good hygiene includes physical, mental, emotional and spiritual health habits for wellness.

• The Fifth Commandment requires that you take good care of your health.

LESSON 6: Choose Life

• Maturity involves making good moral choices for health and life.

• Substance abuse has dangerous and destructive effects on the mind, body and spirit.

• Through prayer, you can receive the grace necessary to resist temptation to damage your health and life.

Thinking It Through

1. What makes you a beautiful person?

2. What does God see in all people that some people in our culture do not?

3. What seems to be a strong temptation in your life right now to use: alcohol, tobacco or drugs?

Matching It Up

On each line, write the letter of the description in Column B that best goes with the term in Column A.

 A

1. E Addiction

2. D Hygiene

3. A Prudence

4. C Nutrition

5. B Temptation

 B

A. Virtue that guides and strengthens us to use drugs appropriately

B. Lure of evil or weakness of will

C. Study of foods and how the human body uses them

D. Practices of cleanliness that promotes good health

E. The mental or physical craving for or dependence on a substance

REVIEWING UNIT 3

Name...

Recalling Key Concepts

Circle the T if the statement is true. Circle the F if the statement is false.

1. An addictive substance is abused because it is illegal.   T   **(F)**
2. God is the source of beauty.   **(T)**   F
3. Wellness is soundness of body and of general physical health.   **(T)**   F
4. Addictive substances can produce a short-term "good" and then bondage.   **(T)**   F
5. Basic physical health care begins with soap and water.   **(T)**   F

Fill in the missing words in these sentences.

6. ....**CIRRHOSIS**........ is a liver disease that prevents the liver from removing harmful substances from the blood and is commonly caused by alcohol abuse.

7. ....**ALCOHOL**........ impairs a person, making it difficult to function and make decisions.

8. ....**PERSPIRATION**........ when mixed with bacteria can develop an unpleasant body odor.

9. The abuse of drugs is contrary to the ....**FIFTH**.......... Commandment.

10. ....**TOBACCO**........ contains a highly addictive substance called nicotine.

Working Together

As a class, create commandments for an abuse-free school. Come up with helpful and effective strategies that will speak to the minds and hearts of students to resist the temptations of using alcohol, tobacco and other substances that will harm them. Vote as a class on the ten most valuable suggestions. Print them on a large poster and display it in the halls for the whole school to see.

44   Unit 3 Review

Recalling Key Concepts

▶ Use this section to help the students be able to accurately recall the key concepts presented in the unit.

▶ For the true and false section, you can have students correct any false statements.

▶ To help with the fill-in-the-blank section, you might want to provide a word bank on the board.

Working Together

▶ Choose a project that best fits the needs and abilities of your students, as well as your time schedule.

▶ Time permitting, have students complete the unit assessment individually or as a class; otherwise, encourage them to complete it at home.

Teaching Tip

Accepting Love: Take this opportunity to help students build self-confidence and a sense of self-worth. Understanding and accepting that God loves them and that they are created in his image and likeness is the foundation for self-love. Because God loves us first, we experience love and can begin to love ourselves. The gift of God's grace can help a person deal with the challenges in life. If some of the youth have already given in to the temptations of living a dangerous life, they should know that you respect them as a child of God, honor their privacy and are sensitive to their struggles. It is never too late to repent for poor choices and with God's grace, to choose a new path.

UNIT 4
God's Gift of Love

Background

"Love of God and love of neighbor are . . . inseparable, they form one single commandment. But both live from the love of God who has loved us first. No longer is it a question, then, of a 'commandment' imposed from without and calling for the impossible, but rather a freely-bestowed experience of love from within, a love which by its very nature must then be shared with others. Love grows through love. Love is 'divine' because it comes from God and ties us to God; through this unifying process it makes us a 'we' which transcends our division and makes us one, until in the end God is 'all in all' " (Deus Caritas Est *18).*

WE ARE CREATED TO BE LOVED AND TO LOVE. THERE is a deep hunger within each of us for love. Pope Benedict XVI in his first encyclical, chose to write on love under the title "God Is Love." This is the very name of God revealed in the New Testament (see John 4:8). God is *agape* or love. The love of God flows out to all creation and especially to humankind.

Both the writings of recent popes and theologians have emphasized a renewed understanding and appreciation of God as Trinity. The interpersonal attraction we experience within us is there because it is from God, in whose image and likeness we have been created. Love is part of our giftedness.

Unfortunately much of what is described as love in contemporary society is self-centered, and not self-giving. It is feeling-based and not rooted in an affection and service to others. The distorted view of love promoted by popular culture is often contrary to the Church's teaching. God reveals that the true nature of human love is an image of divine love. Because of society's misrepresentation of human love, a central part of the Church's educational efforts is directed to clarifying and supporting the life of love between each of us and God. We are to love with intelligence and chastity in accord with our vocational state in life. Otherwise, we will not achieve the deep loving unity to which God invites all.

MESSAGES OF CHASTITY AND ABSTINENCE TO THE youth need to be heard not only from the Church but modeled within families. Adolescents are dealing with the attraction toward members of the complementary gender (other sex). This is a natural part of their development as they mature into adulthood.

The practice of the virtues of chastity and modesty can help young people integrate a Christ-centered balance and control into their lives. This, in turn, can serve as the foundation for their life-long relationships with others. "[C]hastity truly consists in the long-term integration of one's thoughts, feelings, and actions in a way that values, esteems, and respects the dignity of oneself and others" (*Human Sexuality* page 19). The practice of these virtues needs to be presented not simply by saying no, but by choosing to be their own person—to be strong and proud of themselves as persons created by God out of love and for love.

> ### Additional Background
>
> *Catechism of the Catholic Church:* §§ 1642, 1660, 1654, 2348–2350, 2365, 2368

We all have grown up in a culture that offers quite a variety of approaches to love. Every movie we watch, every television program that deals with interpersonal life, will have its own way of portraying love. One way of deepening our own understanding is to watch the media with a critical eye, discerning the differences between authentic love and fraudulent love. This is something that challenges us throughout our lifetime.

For Reflection

Read and reflect on the following:

"Woven through every search for genuine love, for personal maturity, and for interpersonal commitments, is a call to be chaste, sexually responsible, and appropriate for one's particular vocation or state in life" (Human Sexuality *page 19).*

▶ How might the shows I regularly watch impact my understanding and practice of the virtues of chastity and modesty in my personal life?

▶ How might I become aware of the shows my students watch and respond to the messages of those programs into the lesson?

Child Safety

One of the developmental tasks of adolescents is learning how to express affection appropriately. This difficult task has been further complicated by the availability and unsupervised use of social networking sites and electronic communication. Where once young teens worried about holding hands, dancing, and first kisses, now they also are confronted with Internet pornography and sexually explicit electronic messages. This unit will help students identify and develop appropriate responses to temptations and inappropriate requests.

 Family Time

Partnering with the Family

How does each family express love. Some families are very warm and emotional about expressing love while others are more reserved. But every family will have its own ways of saying, "I love you." Invite each family to discuss its own special ways of saying, expressing and "doing" love. Encourage parents to review the corresponding materials available in the Parent Connection, and use the Family Time pages for this unit to discuss the importance of virtuously living a loving life.

Goal: To discover the depth and breadth of love, in which God is the source and initiator of the call for us to love him and one another

Engage
Page 81

Objective
To discover how love transforms a person

Family Time
Ensure that each student tears out their Family Time page to complete at home.

Pray
Act of Love

Focus
List "loves" in life.

Discover
Discuss how love is an act of the heart that can change us.

Teach
Page 82

Objective
To understand the basic meaning of love

Focus
Identify distinctive ways we express love.

Explore
Read, discuss and summarize the three major types of love in human relationships.
Catholics Believe: Trinitarian love is the source of our love.

Connect
Growing in Virtue: Charity is to love as God loves.
Make a montage reflecting the three types of relational love.

Apply
Page 84

Objective
To reflect on the qualities of love as experienced by adolescents

Focus
Imagination exercise

Discover
Catholic Family Album: Pope Benedict XVI

Integrate
Identify the qualities of love using I Corinthians 13:1–13.

Pray
I Corinthians 13:1–13

Vocabulary Preview

Affection—a basic and tender attachment or fondness for another; love in friendship and for neighbor

Charity—the love of human beings for one another because of one's love of God

Love—to will the good of another

Sacrifice—giving up something for someone else's good

Spousal Love—the unique expression of love between a husband and a wife who freely give their whole self to each other; conjugal love

Materials Needed

▶ writing paper
▶ pens, pencils
▶ art supplies
▶ materials for a thank you card
▶ Bible
▶ Lesson 7 Activity Masters

Call to Prayer

God, teach us each day the lessons of love. Help us to love more fearlessly, more openly, more generously. Show us the effects of your love through changed hearts, healed wounds and renewed courage. Amen.

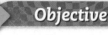
Love Is

Love Works for Change

The fragrance of orange blossoms filled the air. Bells rang. "Isn't Kate beautiful?" Elizabeth whispered to Louise as Katharine entered the chapel. Dressed in a white lace gown, white veil and diamond jewelry, Kate was radiant.

"Yes," Louise whispered back, "she is beautiful. But most of all she is happy—really happy."

Her sisters understood what Kate was doing. But some relatives did not. "Why can't she just go on giving some of her money to charity, as she always has done? Why does she have to enter a convent?" they asked.

Kate had asked herself these questions, too. Her heart told her that the only way to show her love for Jesus and his children was to give herself, her whole life, and not just her money. The archbishop asked Kate what was her desire. In a clear voice she answered, "I wish to start a new congregation of sisters. We will devote ourselves to the care of the Native Americans and to people of color."

Many women joined Kate's religious community. They traveled by stagecoach along dusty roads to remote Native American missions. They traveled to small southern communities to start new schools. Yes, Kate was very happy.

Katharine Drexel grew up in a wealthy Philadelphia banking family. She and her sisters were taught that it is a privilege to share the gifts of God with others. She came to care most for those who had the least.

As the founder of the Sisters of the Blessed Sacrament, Mother Drexel spent over twenty million dollars of her own money to build and run missions and schools. Her love was so great that she is now revered as Saint Katharine Drexel.

> **This lesson will help you to:**
> - **explore** how love transforms a person.
> - **understand** the meaning of love.
> - **reflect** on and practice the qualities of love as experienced in your own life.

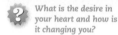
What is the desire in your heart and how is it changing you?

Love Is   47

Objective

To discover how love transforms a person

Pray

Open the lesson with the prayer, an Act of Love.

Focus

Write on the board: I Love . . . Then have students list in two minutes a list of their "loves." Ask if their listed items fall into common categories, such as food, material objects, people, etc.

Discover

▶ Read, "Love Works for Change." Invite students to speculate on St. Katharine's list of loves.

▶ Explain: We often identify that which we love as coming from our heart.

▶ Inquire: What is a desire in your heart and how does it affect you?

▶ Discuss how the desires of the heart can change us.

▶ Time permitting, see if students can identify a model of Christian love, like St. Katharine Drexel, and explain why they chose that person. Note the person need not be a canonized saint to model love.

Teaching Tip

Attitudes of the World: Before concluding this lesson on love, be sure that you have taken the time to examine your students' various ways of understanding what love is. In this examination give attention to the similarities and differences between a person's understanding of love depending on their age. Point out how our attitudes toward love change as we mature because of how our relationships develop. Recognizing the needs of the one loved is a sign of maturity. This attitude can lead to sacrificial love. Allow students to discover the various and sometimes contradictory attitudes toward love in popular culture. Praise the students for their witness to Christian love, especially when it calls for sacrifice.

Objective

To understand the basic meaning of love

Focus

Using the list of the students' loves, challenge them to define love in each context. See if they would define love in the same way for different things. For example, loving food and loving people would not mean the same kind of love.

Explore

▶ Have students quietly read "The Meaning of Love." Then as a class read the text aloud, pausing for students to react or ask questions.

▶ Write on the board the three types of love: friendship, marriage and charity. Ask: Is there any other kind of love? *(Yes, but these three focus on relationships).*

▶ Read the Catholics Believe box. Explain that the Church focuses on the types of love in relationships because this is how we understand God and ourselves.

▶ Using the chart on the board, have students list examples for each type of love and the way in which that love is shown and experienced.

▶ Ask students to identify the ways that each type of love is expressed appropriately. For example, friends show love by doing kind things for each other, parents show love for their children by caring for them, etc.

Catholics Believe

God created each person out of love and for love. Our basic vocation in life is to love one another as God loves us. Our loving relationships are to reflect the loving communion of three Divine Persons in one God, the Trinity (CCC 212, 1022–1024, 1337, and 1604).

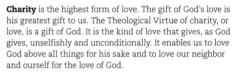

The Meaning of Love

The more you love, the more you grow in love. Each time you give love, you have more to give. Love can never be used up. Love, at its heart and in all forms, is to will the good of another. Love is a word that is often misused in our society. In reality there are many types of love.

Friendship is a form of love. Mary Beth and Monica enjoy being together. They get along easily, and they have a lot in common. They are like sisters. When either one has something to share, she immediately calls the other. Mary Beth and Monica share the affectionate bond of good friends. Affection involves attachment and closeness. You could feel this kind of love for anyone: a sibling, a neighbor or a friend.

Marriage is a form of love. As David and Sarah dated, they knew they wanted to be together constantly. What started out as a romantic love matured into their desire to be married. David and Sarah had fallen in love and desired to love one another faithfully and exclusively. They recognized that their strong feelings and sexual attraction for each other needed a lifelong commitment. This is the kind of mature and intimate love shared between a husband and a wife who have made a lifelong commitment to one another.

Charity is the highest form of love. The gift of God's love is his greatest gift to us. The Theological Virtue of charity, or love, is a gift of God. It is the kind of love that gives, as God gives, unselfishly and unconditionally. It enables us to love God above all things for his sake and to love our neighbor and ourself for the love of God.

Real charity calls for sacrifice. Sacrifice means giving up something for someone else's good. For example, after college Patty decided to serve the poor in Cambodia. She had the type of love that could give with no strings attached. Patty's sacrifices for the people in Cambodia flowed from her love of God. Charity is the kind of love that gives unselfishly and unconditionally.

 Think about the different aspects of love you have experienced.

48   Love Is

Teaching Tip

In Other Words: Students might enjoy knowing the word *love* in different languages. Write on the board the Greek words for love and teach them how to pronounce them: *storḡe* (stohr-GAY) refers to affection, like within the family; *philia* (FEE-lee-ah) refers to love between friends, usually reflected in loyalty; *eros* (AIR-ohs) refers to passionate desire, most often associated with romantic or spousal love; *agape* (Ah-gah-pay) refers to charity, an unconditional love for another person. Have students research other cultural distinctions or words for love to help facilitate a discussion on the meaning of love. Note also that C. S. Lewis wrote the book, *The Four Loves*, from a Christian perspective to elaborate on the four types of love based on the Greek distinctions.

As you can see, a person is capable of experiencing and expressing their love in several ways. Christian love in all its forms is self-giving love. It is the love that Jesus had for his Father and shared with his disciples, "As the Father loves me, so I also love you" (John 15:9). It is the love Jesus commands his disciples to live. "This is my commandment: love one another as I love you. No one has greater love than this, to lay down one's life for one's friends" (John 15:12–13). The First Letter of John sums it up this way: "Beloved, let us love one another, because love is of God; everyone who loves is begotten by God . . . for God is love" (1 John 4:7–8).

Growing in Virtue

In order to love another, I must love myself. To love myself requires accepting God's love of me. Love can never be used up if that love comes from God who is the source of all love. To love as God loves is **charity**.

"Montage of Love"

Create an image montage of the three types of love discussed in this lesson. Be sure to represent God's love in the center because it is the source for all.

Love Is   49

▶ Ask students how they would feel if an acquaintance started showing affection that was appropriate only in a marriage? What should they do in this situation? Explain that they should express their discomfort, ask the person to stop, move away and tell a trusted adult what happened.

Connect

▶ Inquire: How do you know that you love someone or they love you?

▶ Read the Growing in Virtue box. Then have students gather in their small groups and discuss why love can grow and never be used up.

▶ Have students complete the activity on the page. If needed, have them finish the activity at home with their family. Be sure to monitor the appropriateness of images used for the activity.

▶ Time permitting, allow students to research quotes in the Bible about love. Consider using a Bible concordance to find Scripture passages that include the word *love*.

Extending the Lesson

Using Activity Master 7A: Use the Activity Master "What's the Message." This activity provides students an opportunity to further examine the different types of meanings for love.

Popular Love: The second part of Activity Master 7A asks students to identify examples of love from popular culture, such as music, advertisement and television. Allow ample time for students to research or come up with these examples. You can also have them create their own lyrics, slogans or messages that reflect a healthy meaning of love in its appropriate relationship.

Objective

To reflect on the qualities of love as experienced by adolescents

Focus

Have students imagine that Jesus spent an entire day at their school. Have them discuss what he might smile at, frown upon, wonder about or laugh with you about. List the situations on the board as appropriate expressions of love or violations of love.

Discover

Read the Catholic Family Album. Ask: Why is love central to Christianity? *(God is love; we are created to love and Christ shows us the way to love.)*

Integrate

▶ Read, "Choosing to Live the Way of Love." Discuss what doing good without love means. For example, doing good without love is like helping a neighbor begrudgingly.

▶ Have students complete the activity on the page. They should complete the chart individually and then pair up to compare responses. Invite the groups to share examples from their life with the whole class.

Pray

Invite students to pray using I Corinthians 13:1–13 as inspiration for thanking God for revealing to us the many aspects of love.

Catholic Family Album

Pope Benedict XVI wrote his first encyclical on love. It is called *Deus Caritas Est* (God Is Love). An encyclical is a letter written by a pope to the bishops and the whole Church that contains an official explanation of the Church's teaching. In "God Is Love" Pope Benedict explains that every form of love, to be genuine, must first be rooted in divine love. Every human expression of love should be an image of God's love. Every human relationship should be nourished by love, first divine and then human. He explains that at the heart of Christianity is love because God is love and created each of us out of love and for love.

Choosing to Live the Way of Love

In one of his letters, Saint Paul speaks of a "more excellent way" of life. That more excellent way is the way of love. Saint Paul teaches the early Church in Corinth that if we do good things, but do them without love, our actions are meaningless.

Read Saint Paul's description of the qualities of love in 1 Corinthians 13:1–13. Then tell what each quality listed below means in your own words. Finally, give a real life example of how you will try to live the "more excellent way" Paul teaches.

LOVE IS . . .	MEANING	I WILL
Patient		
Kind		
Not jealous		
Not pompous or inflated		
Not rude		
Not self-seeking		
Not quick tempered		

50   Love Is

Extending the Lesson

Using Activity Master 7B: Use the Activity Master "Love in Action." This activity provides a list of organizations that work to serve people in need. Then ask students to write a letter to one of the organizations.

Faith in Action: Since love is central to Christianity, our faith demands of us to live our love in action. Have students list ways they can put their faith into action through charitable practical acts. These acts can reflect the Beatitudes or Works of Mercy or promote social justice in other ways.

Activity Master 7A

Name

What's the Message?

We often use the word "love" when we mean lots of other things. What are we really saying? (Example: "I love a roller coaster" means "I enjoy the sensation of riding on a roller coaster.")

1. Translate the following messages to show their real meanings.

Message	Translation
I love your sweater.	
I love spaghetti.	
I love that TV sitcom.	
I love baseball.	
I love purple.	

2. Think of a song, and advertisement, and a television show that include the word "love." Write down what you heard, then translate the message.

Message	Translation
Song	
Advertisement	
TV Show	

© RCL Publishing LLC

Family Life Grade 7

Activity Master 7B

Name

Love in Action

Below is a list of organizations that work to serve people in need. In small groups with your classmates, think of some questions you have about the organization assigned to you. Then write a letter to the organization, asking your questions and requesting additional information. (What can you, your family, and your friends do to support them?)

Caritas Internationalis
Palazzo San Calisto
Vatican City State
V-00120
http://www.caritas.org

Catholic Campaign for Human Development
3211 4th Street, N.E.
Washington DC 20017-1194
http://www.usccb.org/cchd

Catholic Charities USA
Sixty-Six Canal Center Plaza, Suite 600
Alexandria, VA 22314
http://www.catholiccharitiesusa.org

Catholic Coalition on Climate Change
P.O. Box 60205
Washington DC 20039
http://www.catholicsandclimatechange.org

Catholic Health Association of the United States
1875 Eye Street NW, Suite 1000
Washington DC 20006-5440
http://www.chausa.org

Catholic Relief Services
228 W. Lexington Street
Baltimore, Maryland 21201-3413
http://www.crs.org

Cultural Orientation Resource Center
Center for Applied Linguistics
4646 40th Street, NW
Washington DC 20016-1859
http://www.cal.org/co

Justice for Immigrants
3211 4th Street, N.E.
Washington DC 20017-1194
http://www.justiceforimmigrants.org

Migration & Refugee Services
3211 4th Street, N.E.
Washington DC 20017-1194
http://www.usccb.org/mrs

National Domestic Violence Hotline
P.O. Box 161810
Austin, Texas 78716
http://www.ndvh.org

© RCL Publishing LLC

Family Life Grade 7

How to Find It
How to Use It

Step 1: Click & Select

Go to RCLBFamilyLife.com
Click on the link for activities.
Then select the activity master you need.

Step 2: Print & Copy

Print each activity master in advance.
Then copy enough for everyone in the class.

Step 3: Share & Discuss

Once students have completed the activity,
have them share and discuss their responses.

Goal: To understand the role of attraction in human relationships and how chastity integrates sexuality into the life and love of human relationships

Engage
Page 87

Objective
To understand the role of attraction in relationships

Pray
Prayer of thanksgiving

Focus
Explain how our commonalities influence attraction.

Discover
Facilitate a discussion on the importance of time and work in our relationships.

Teach
Page 88

Objective
To examine and understand the importance of chastity

Focus
Practice patience in silence; Ecclesiastes 3:1–15

Explore
Read, discuss and summarize why every relationship needs chastity in order to grow in health and holiness.
Catholics Believe: Chastity as a spiritual power
Growing in Virtue: Chastity as a moral virtue

Connect
Analyze a music video on its portrayal of love.

Apply
Page 90

Objective
To address the pressures of becoming sexually active

Focus
List pressures to become sexually active.

Discover
Catholic Family Album: Saint Josemaria Escriva

Integrate
Examine how a person handles pressures in life.

Pray
Pray for grace to live chastely.

Reviewing Unit 4
Summarize and review the content from both lessons.

Vocabulary Preview

Attraction—the sense of being drawn to or pulled toward something or someone; in relationships feelings of warmth, trust, care and generosity are experienced

Chastity—the successful integration of the gift of sexuality within the whole person, flows from the cardinal virtue of temperance

Conjugal Love—the unique expression of sexual love between a husband and wife who give to each other their whole self as a gift

Sexual Attraction—attraction to another person based on their gender; part of God's plan to help a man and a woman become husband and wife

Materials Needed

▶ writing paper
▶ pens, pencils
▶ art supplies
▶ timer
▶ Bible
▶ Lesson 8 Activity Masters

Call to Prayer

Lord, you have given us the gift of sexuality. Help us to respect one another and to express our sexuality according to your will. Guide my students in patience, trusting in your plan for each one of them. Help them to appreciate the joys and responsibilities in the gift of their sexuality. Amen.

Chastity

The Power of Attraction

Think about your friends and the groups you have chosen to belong to. When you think about it, friendships and belonging to a group results from being "attracted" to them.

At its basic level, attraction includes feelings of comfort, warmth, trust, care and generosity. This basic attraction draws you to form friendships with people of both sexes and of all ages. The attraction we experience with our friends, siblings and neighbors is part of the enjoyment we have with them. This attraction is based on familiarity with and genuine concern for the people whom you desire to be around. You feel happy and comfortable being with them, and they enjoy being with you. God created us this way.

Responding appropriately to the attraction we feel toward others takes work. It takes time and effort. For example, the desire to be with a friend is not enough to sustain the friendship. You know that you have to work at being a friend. Just like studying for a test, practicing for the big game or rehearsing for the concert, maintaining close relationships appropriately takes commitment and sacrifice.

This truth is already in your heart. For the power of attraction to have an effect, you must love beyond self-gratifying feelings. Sometimes you must choose to love even on those days when you do not feel like it. Sometimes truly being a friend and loving someone requires you to say no. And when you do, you still love them.

Friendships, marriages and every kind of loving relationship includes a power of attraction that involves choosing to love for the sake of the other. This is God's plan for loving relationships. This is the way Jesus taught us how God loves and how we are to love.

This lesson will help you to:

- **explore** the role of attraction in human relationships.
- **examine** and understand the importance of chastity in human relationships.
- **address** the pressures of becoming sexually active.

 How do you choose to show your attraction toward your friends?

Chastity 51

Teaching Tip

Chastity Versus Abuse: Chastity promotes a healthy and holy use of one's sexuality; abuse debases one's sexuality. People who have been abused fear that they will forever be considered unlovable and undesirable, that no one will want "damaged goods." Abuse deeply wounds the victim's self-image. The emphasis in this lesson focuses on helping students understand that God created everyone good and that goodness can never be destroyed, no matter what is done to them. Abuse victims need reassurance that they have done nothing wrong, but that wrong was done to them; that the abuse did not make them dirty or bad, but that terrible things were done to them. They have not lost their dignity; they are still lovable and good.

Objective

To understand the role of attraction in relationships

Pray

Open the lesson giving thanks to God for creating us to live in loving relationships.

Focus

Have students list what they share in common with their closest friends. Explain that these common things reveal an attraction. What we like in common brings us together.

Discover

► Read "The Power of Attraction." Clarify: Attraction is the simple human need to be with others we like and trust. Every relationship involves attraction.

► Have students imagine what it would be like if they always had their favorite food available for them to consume. What might result in the over-indulgence of eating it?

► Explain that growing and achieving a goal that is worthwhile takes time and work; for example, becoming an Olympian, a great musician, etc.

► Have students identify examples of commitment and sacrifice with their friends.

Objective

To examine and understand the importance of chastity

Focus

▶ Set a timer for two minutes. Have students sit without moving or speaking until the timer goes off. Discuss the difficulties in this exercise.

▶ Have students discuss which tastes better instant food or slow-cooked food; for example, microwaved beef or slow-roasted brisket.

▶ Inquire: What is the benefit of allowing something to mature over time?

▶ Read aloud for the class Ecclesiastes 3:1–15. Ask students for examples from their own lives when patience paid off.

Explore

▶ Have students quietly read the text on the page. Then encourage reactions and questions.

▶ Help students connect maturing over time with the virtue of chastity. Explain that time gives us the opportunity to know others and ourselves better.

▶ Read the Catholics Believe box. Explain that living the virtue of chastity includes patience and expressing affection appropriately in relationships.

▶ Inquire: Why does every relationship need chastity?

▶ Define sexual abuse, referring to content in Teaching Tip on this page.

Catholics Believe

The chaste person maintains the integrity of the powers of life and love placed within him or her. Chastity ensures the unity of the whole person by protecting the integrity of both the body and soul. Jesus is the model of chastity (CCC 2338, 2345).

Choosing to Love

As you mature, your relationships will change. You might realize that your desire to hang out with your friends is increasing. In addition, as a person matures physically, mentally, emotionally and spiritually, their sexual attraction for a person of the other gender increases. As the body systems develop, hormones are released causing a mixture of feelings within us. Feelings within a friendship might also include sexual attraction. This is healthy and part of how God made us to be in relationships.

The virtue of chastity helps us to integrate God's gift of sexuality within us. Living a chaste life is about directing our sexuality toward authentic love. It is not about repressing sexual feelings. Chastity is part of every kind of relationship. It is the virtue that allows us to do what is right, good and truly loving in every relationship.

One way we live the virtue of chastity is through the practice of abstinence. Abstinence is choosing to say no to all forms of sexual activity. Since God gave us the gift of sexual attraction to help lead a man and a woman to share their love in marriage, intimate sexual activity is reserved for marriage. God's plan for marriage requires both spouses to commit to a lifelong relationship based on fidelity, exclusivity and openness to life. Abstinence, then, helps a person to honor God's plan for marriage.

 Think about why every relationship needs chastity to be healthy and loving.

52   Chastity

Teaching Tip

Models of Modesty: Provide opportunities for students to discuss modesty, which is also a form of temperance. Modesty is temperance in the way we present ourselves in dress, behavior and speech. Help students see that, like chastity, modesty respects the person and builds confidence in oneself. Guide them in identifying persons that they regard as models of modesty. Emphasize modesty in demeanor, attitude and attire. Modesty is often accompanied by self-acceptance, humility and honesty.

Child Safety: Sexual is abuse is wrong, not because sex is dirty or bad, but because a person in a position of power is taking advantage of another person. Offenders can be adults or other children. Sexual abuse is never the victim's fault.

Conjugal Love

In marriage sexual attraction is expressed in many ways but especially through sexual intercourse. Once a man and woman have married, they can express their love through sexual intercourse. This is part of spousal love, also called conjugal love. Spousal love is the unique expression between a husband and wife as each gives to the other their whole self as a gift. This is why spouses are to love one another completely, faithfully and exclusively. This is the commitment and sacrifice that marriage requires. Conjugal love is the love uniting a husband and wife in marriage.

God created you to be in loving relationships. When we will the good of another, we offer self-giving love. He also gave you the gift of free will to choose what is good and right. Your free will gives you the power to be free from selfishness and to love another with genuine concern, compassion, acceptance, generosity and a spirit of sacrifice.

Growing in Virtue

Chastity is a moral virtue, a grace from God and one of the Fruits of the Holy Spirit. Chastity allows a person to do what is right, good and truly loving in every kind of relationship. When we live chaste lives, we respect others as persons and not as objects to be used.

"Lyrics of Love"

In a small group discuss how music videos encourage or discourage people to live a chaste live and to love one another as Jesus taught us to love. Rewrite a song to encourage chaste living.

Activity

Chastity 53

▶ Read the Growing in Virtue box. Ask: What does it mean to use someone like an object and not treat and respect them as a person? Explain that people are not to love others like they "love" things. A person is to be respected for who they are not for what they do or what they look like.

▶ Point out that chastity also refers to how a person acts in public: in real or virtual life. Have students offer examples of how they think a chaste person would act in person or online in a social network.

▶ Review Internet safety rules. What is appropriate to post online? Discuss why "sexts," sexually explicit messages or photos, are wrong. Have students make up a list of steps that they should take when they are exposed to sexually explicit materials. Post rules in the classroom.

Connect

▶ Explain: Chastity enables one to respect another as a person and not use them like an object. Inquire: How is chastity not repression of desire but integration of love?

▶ Have students complete the activity on the page. If needed, have them finish the activity at home with their family.

▶ Time permitting, discuss violations of chastity and the varying degrees of gravity; for example, immodest dress, pornography, rape, incest, masturbation, adultery, cohabitation, contraception, polygamy, homosexual activity and sexual abuse.

Extending the Lesson

Using Activity Master 8A: Use the Activity Master "Handling Sexual Attraction." This activity is an opportunity for students to develop healthy ways to handle strong feelings, such as sexual attraction, by reflecting on and evaluating hypothetical situations.

Consequences: Without over-emphasizing the consequences of inappropriate sexual activity, students should be informed of the risks involved. Have a professional health-care provider speak on the topic of sexually transmitted diseases. Be sure that pregnancy is not presented as an equivalent consequence to these diseases, nor contraception as a morally acceptable means of prevention. Abstinence is part of chastity and thus a moral and healthy way to avoid sexually transmitted diseases.

Objective

To address the pressures of becoming sexually active

Focus

▶ Separate the boys and girls. Divide them into small groups to create a list of pressures youth their age feel to become sexually active. (Note: Emphasize that the youth are to name cultural pressures. This is not to be a revelation of personal experiences.)

▶ Discuss as a whole class their lists, noticing differences and similarities.

Discover

Read the Catholic Family Album. Ask: How did St. Josemaria deal with difficulties? *(He centered his life on Christ, prayed and lived virtuously.)*

Integrate

▶ Read "Responding to Pressure." Discuss how students feel and what they do when under pressure.

▶ Remind students that they can always speak to their parents or another trusted adult about the pressures they feel and how they should respond.

▶ Have students complete the activity on the page. As a class decide what is the greatest pressure, its source and how to respond in a virtuous way.

Pray

Ask for the grace to find the strength to live chastely.

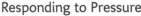

Catholic Family Album

Saint Josemaria Escriva (1902–1975) spoke of virtuous living constantly. He said, "Chastity is the triumphant affirmation of love." Josemaria saw Christ as a great model for chaste living. Despite the suffering he faced, Josemaria wanted to love as God loves, in a spirit of sacrifice. He helped others see how their daily life could be an act of love for God and others.

Responding to Pressure

Whistling teakettles work under pressure. The whistling is a clear signal that the water in the kettle is boiling. Whistling is an appropriate response to the pressure inside the kettle. Each day Christians face internal and external "pressures" to live or not to live a chaste life. How can you possibly respond to those pressures?

Like any pressure in life, you must understand the situation and take control. Sometimes this is difficult. Remember that the guidance and grace of the Holy Spirit are always with you. Prayer and the regular reception of the Sacraments of the Eucharist and Penance and Reconciliation will give you the strength to live a chaste life.

Use the chart below to identify the pressures that come from each source and how you can commit to living a chaste life.

SOURCE	HOW IT PRESSURES	MY CHASTE RESPONSE
Peers		
Parents		
Media		
Church		

54   Chastity

Extending the Lesson

Using Activity Master 8B: Use the Activity Master "The Language of Clothes." This activity gives students an opportunity to think about some of the messages communicated with the clothes a person wears.

Tips to Diffuse Pressure: Practice healthy strategies for diffusing pressure. Examples include humor, changing the subject, saying no, leaving the scene or avoiding the situation in anticipation. Pair up students to write and role-play a scenario to show both healthy and unhealthy ways to respond when one is pressured to do something that is morally wrong or that the person just doesn't want to do. Encourage the class to offer suggestions as the scenario plays out.

Activity Master 8A

Name ....

Handling Sexual Attraction

As a young child, you learned to handle strong feelings like anger, fear, and sadness by talking and praying about them. Now you're learning to handle another emotion: sexual attraction. Write some ideas about handling each of these situations.

1. Sandra says:
"Josh and I have been friends since first grade. We've always had a special kind of understanding for each other. But now, we're feeling something more than friendship. It's wonderful, but I don't want to go with him and he does. I'm afraid if I tell him how I feel, I'll hurt his feelings and it will completely break up our relationship."

_____

_____

_____

_____

_____

_____

2. Mark says:
"Some of my friends like to hang around the halls at school and yell at the girls as they go by. It's not just flirting; their remarks are really embarrassing. One of the guys said, 'Don't worry, the girls like it.' I'm feeling totally uncomfortable. But if I say anything, they'll think I'm immature or trying to be holy, or something. I might lose my friends."

_____

_____

_____

_____

_____

_____

_____

Family Life Grade 7

© RCL Publishing LLC

Activity Master 8B

Name ....

The Language of Clothes

John T. Molloy, author of *Dress for Success*, found that what we wear can send out strong messages. For example, inappropriate clothing can turn off a prospective employer, and an unconventional uniform can destroy a patient's confidence in a doctor or nurse. Think about some messages you've read in other people's clothing. Then think what messages your clothes send.

1. Have you ever seen clothing (on people of any age) that sent the following messages? Tell what the outfits were like.

"Look at me! Look at me!"

_____

"I don't care what anybody thinks."

_____

"I want to look like someone I admire."

_____

"I want you to know how I'm feeling."

_____

"I want to look sexy."

_____

"I want to look a different age than I actually am."

_____

2. Write two messages you think your clothes might have delivered at different times.

a. _____

b. _____

Family Life Grade 7

© RCL Publishing LLC

How to Find It
How to Use It

Step 1: Click & Select

Go to RCLBFamilyLife.com
Click on the link for activities.
Then select the activity master you need.

Step 2: Print & Copy

Print each activity master in advance.
Then copy enough for everyone in the class.

Step 3: Share & Discuss

Once students have completed the activity,
have them share and discuss their responses.

REVIEWING UNIT 4

Summary

▶ Ask the students to read through the Summary section.

▶ Invite them to ask questions about any points that are not clear to them.

▶ Make sure to expand on any points that were perhaps touched on only lightly during class time.

Thinking It Through

▶ Have students answer all three questions on the page.

▶ Assign each student a number from one through three.

▶ Have students share with the class their answer to the question that corresponds to their assigned number.

Matching It Up

Use this matching section to help the students identify the appropriate definition or description of a key concept, term or person from the unit.

Name ....

Summary

Remember what you have learned in each of the lessons in God's Gift of Love.

LESSON 7: Love Is

- There are different aspects of love according to our relationships. Love is expressed either as friends, neighbors, spouses or as charity.
- St. Paul provides us a description of the qualities of love from which we can examine our own experiences of love.

LESSON 8: Chastity

- Sexual attraction is a natural feeling and a gift in God's plan for a man and a woman to become husband and wife.
- Chastity integrates God's gift of sexuality within us, respecting each other as persons.
- Through chaste living we can respond to the pressures of becoming sexually active through healthy and holy choices.

Thinking It Through

1. List ways in which you desire to be treated with respect by others of the complementary or other sex.

2. What pressures do you feel about maturing sexually? How can you best deal with them?

3. List examples of chaste living.

Matching It Up

On each line, write the letter of the description in Column B that best goes with the term in Column A.

A

1. __D__ Affection

2. __E__ Charity

3. __B__ Chastity

4. __C__ Conjugal love

5. __A__ Sacrifice

B

A. Giving up something for someone else's good

B. The successful integration of the gift of sexuality

C. The unique love between husband and wife

D. A simple and tender attachment or fondness

E. The love of human beings for one another that comes from God's love

Unit 4 Review   55

REVIEWING UNIT 4

REVIEWING UNIT 4

Name...

Recalling Key Concepts

Circle the T if the statement is true. Circle the F if the statement is false.

1. Charity involves sacrifice.   (T)   F
2. Chastity only applies to those who are not married.   T   (F)
3. God's gift of sexual attraction is to help a man and a woman become husband and wife.   (T)   F
4. Friendship does not involve attraction.   T   (F)
5. Charity is unconditional love for others inspired by Christ's love.   (T)   F

Fill in the missing words in these sentences.

6. ......**LOVE**...... is to will the good of another.

7. In marriage sexual attraction is expressed through ...**SEXUAL INTERCOURSE**... as an act of love showing a full commitment between spouses as gifts to one another.

8. ...**KATHARINE DREXEL**... was a saint who witnessed charity through her community, Sisters of the Blessed Sacrament.

9. Our basic ...**VOCATION**... in life is to love one another as God loves us.

10. With chastity comes the capacity for compassion, acceptance, generosity and a spirit of ...**SACRIFICE**...

Working Together

Divide into two groups—girls in one group, boys in the other. In each group talk about ways to support one another in being faithful to God's plan for you as you mature sexually. How can you and your classmates be a positive influence on others?

Recalling Key Concepts

▶ Use this section to help the students be able to accurately recall the key concepts from the unit.

▶ For the true and false section, you can have students correct any false statements.

▶ To help with the fill-in-the-blank section, you might want to provide a word bank on the board.

Working Together

▶ Choose a project that best fits the need and abilities of your students, as well as your time schedule.

▶ Time permitting, have students complete the unit assessment individually or as a class; otherwise, encourage them to complete it at home.

Teaching Tip

Wisdom in Prayer: Offer a mini-lesson on the four traditional forms or types of prayer: blessing, petition, thanksgiving and praise (see CCC 2623–2643). Have students focus on prayers from or based on Scripture, especially those found in the Book of Psalms (see CCC 2585–2589). Be sure students are familiar with inspirational definitions of prayers. For example, St. Thérèse of Lisieux called prayer a "surge of the heart" and St. John Damascene called prayer the "raising of one's mind and heart to God" (see CCC 2558–2561). Explain how each type of prayer can be a spiritual expression of maturity. In and through prayer, God helps and transforms us with the power of his grace.

UNIT 5
God's Gift of Community

Background

"As a spiritual being, the human creature is defined through interpersonal relations. The more authentically he or she lives in these relations, the more his or her personal identity matures. It is not by isolation that man establishes his worth, but by placing himself in relation with others and with God. Hence these relations take on fundamental importance" (Caritas in Veritate 53).

THE FAMILY IS THE PRIMARY SCHOOL OF VIRTUE.
This is one of the basic social teachings of the Church. The whole of society rests in some measure on the vitality and the sense of responsibility that is nurtured in the family.

But the family is not an isolated social cell; it is part of the wider society. As children mature, they begin to find important social connections outside their families with friends. This is a wonderful process that should be encouraged. Most children will eventually leave their families of origin and establish their own families. There is a very significant "in-between" period when friendships share with the family, the role of socializing children into adulthood.

At its best, the family nurtures within children interests and leads them to understand and appreciate that community life is good, enriching and necessary. Human beings need experiences in community life to help bring out the best in one another. By participating in community life, a person benefits from the gifts of others and offers their own gifts to others.

MOVEMENT OUTSIDE THE FAMILY CAN BE QUITE
difficult for children and their parents. Personal virtue will be tested. Temptations involving self harm may

surface. A sense of one's own personal dignity may be jeopardized. It is therefore important that parents and teachers combine their efforts to assist the youth through the sometimes rough waters of adolescence.

Some social relationships can be dangerous. Students in seventh grade are beginning to feel the first winds of the hurricane that almost all will eventually face. Deepening their own sense of personal dignity, discussing the real world with all its blessings and difficulties is not wasted effort. In fact, it is crucial that teenagers know what lies ahead so that they can live and love responsibly.

THE WORLD INHABITED BY YOUNG PEOPLE TODAY
has characteristics and challenges different than the world even of a generation ago. As we focus more on friendships in today's world, it is helpful for teachers and parents to learn about the world now inhabited by the youth. As one wise educator once said, we were never their age.

One of the best ways to know the world of others is to have them describe it to us, to give us a tour of their land. This means learning at least a basic knowledge of their culture, their interests, their hopes and their

> ### Additional Background
> *Catechism of the Catholic Church:* §§ 946–962, 1877, 1906, 1912–1916, 1925–1926

fears. One sign of effective teachers is that they are the students of their students. Invite your students to be your teacher. Listen and learn; do not just talk and teach. Try not to be overly critical; your world was once probably quite strange to your parents back in the day.

For Reflection

Read and reflect on the following:

"The family is the community in which, from childhood, one can learn moral values, begin to honor God, and make good use of freedom. Family life is an initiation into life in society" (Catechism of the Catholic Church 2207).

▶ What gifts do I contribute to my family to help them grow as a community and a school of love? How generously do I contribute those gifts?

▶ What gifts do I recognize in each of the students? How might I encourage them to contribute those gifts to the building of the class into a true community?

Child Safety

Chastity is the virtue at the core of child safety education. By practicing the virtue of chastity, children learn what is appropriate behavior regarding sexual expression. By learning what is appropriate behavior, children will then learn to quickly recognize inappropriate or unchaste behavior. Once taught to recognize inappropriate behavior, they can then make informed decisions on what to do in uncomfortable situations and decide quickly how to respond to and report any inappropriate behavior.

Family Time

Partnering with the Family

Religious formation of children is the primary responsibility of parents or guardians. The Family Time pages that begin each unit of *Family Life* help parents and other members of the family fulfill this responsibility. By sending these materials home, you are working in partnership with the parents to help them and their children to continue to grow as a healthy and holy family.

Goal: To examine the impact of our personal actions on society and identify some of the social evils that result from personal sin

Engage
Page 97

Objective
To explore the power and impact of free will

Family Time
Ensure that each student tears out their Family Time page to complete at home.

Pray
Moment of silence, examination of conscience

Focus
Genesis 3:1–24

Discover
Discuss the effects of sin, especially that which violates the truth and meaning of human sexuality.

Teach
Page 98

Objective
To identify some social evils that violate human dignity

Focus
Identify examples of social evils; Ephesians 4:17–32.

Explore
Read, discuss and summarize the social evil that exists in sexual abuse.
Catholics Believe: Self-mastery and chastity

Connect
Growing in Virtue: Informed conscience
Design an advertisement promoting human love as beautiful and sacred.

Apply
Page 100

Objective
To discern the kinds of messages portrayed in the media

Focus
Chart engagement and use of various mass media

Discover
Catholic Family Album: The Samaritan Woman

Integrate
Identify a positive message in popular media

Pray
Prayer of petition

Vocabulary Preview

Cyber-bullying—the misuse of the Internet for the purposes of degrading or demeaning others

Sin—a deliberate thought, word, deed or omission contrary to God's law

Pornography—any efforts to portray real or simulated sexual acts for the use by others that betrays the truth and meaning of human sexuality and demeans persons as objects

Social Evil—the impact of personal sin that influences or includes the sins of others

Social Sin—the effect of sin, over time, which can affect society and its institutions to create "structures of sin"

Materials Needed

▶ writing paper
▶ pens, pencils
▶ art supplies
▶ Bible
▶ Lesson 9 Activity Masters

Call to Prayer
God, you created us out of love and gave us the ability to love one another. Remind us that your Son, Jesus, taught us how to live and showed us the way of love. May your Spirit, dwelling within us, help us to know your love and become loving people. Amen.

Consequences

Created to Share Love

The Bible is the Revelation of what God wants us to know about himself and about ourselves. In the very beginning of the Bible, God tells us that he shared his love generously and unselfishly when he created humankind: "God created man in his image" (Genesis 1:27). But that is only part of the message. That same verse of Scripture contains another very important truth about ourselves. "The Lord God said: 'It is not good for the man be to alone. I will make a suitable partner for him' " (Genesis 2:18).

In other words, God created humankind to live in community. He created us to share our life and love with each other as he shares his life and love with us, generously, unselfishly, in a life-giving way.

God's love for us is so generous and life-giving that he gave us the gift of free will. We can freely accept or freely reject God's love. The Book of Genesis tells the "sad" story of how Adam and Eve chose to use their free will. They turned their backs on God and rejected his love. They used their knowledge and free will selfishly. They sinned.

Because of that first sin, or Original Sin, all people have a tendency to reject God's gift of love. In others words, we tend to sin. Every sin involves a personal choice. Over time, the effect of personal sins can become part of the way society acts. When this happens, personal sins create a way of acting that we call social evil.

When we face choices to take part in social evil, our free will gives us the power to say no. We can reject and walk away from such evil. We can say yes to God.

> **This lesson will help you to:**
> - **explore** the power of our free will.
> - **identify** some social evils that violate human dignity.
> - **discern** the messages about human relationships the media portrays.

 What are some sins and their effects that you see degrading people?

Teaching Tip

Understanding Scripture: As with all Scripture, it is to be read in context and in accordance with the Church's interpretation. Therefore, using a Catholic study Bible with the footnotes and a reader's guide can assist you in explaining the passages to your students. For example, in Genesis 3, God desired for human beings to be able to discern the difference between right and wrong; what human beings don't have is the power to determine what is right and wrong. God alone is the arbiter of moral norms, and he gave us both faith and reason to discern and understand what he has determined. This is the meaning behind the tree in the middle of the garden, the tree of knowledge of good and evil. See Pope John Paul II's *Veritatis Splendor* [Splendor of Truth], 35–37.

Objective

To explore the power and impact of free will

Pray

Open the lesson with a moment of silence and an examination of conscience.

Focus

Read Genesis 3:1–24. Inquire: Why do you think Adam and Eve chose to disobey God's will? Guide them in a proper interpretation of the passages. For example, they put themselves before God; they put their own desires before their love for God.

Discover

▶ Read "Created to Share Love." Ask: How is the Story of Creation a love story? *(one who loves shares, gives gifts and seeks love in return)*

▶ Have students form groups to discuss the effects of Original Sin. *(Some effects of Original Sin are: loss of grace and original holiness, death, suffering, ignorance, sin became universally present in the world.)*

▶ Then have groups discuss how the personal sins of a bully online impact society.

▶ Reinforce the concept of sexuality as the integration of the whole person as God created them to be, male or female. Therefore, sexual abuse can be physical, emotional and mental.

TEACH

Objective

To identify some social evils that violate human dignity

Focus

▶ Have students identify some examples of social evils in the world. Clarify that sin is a personal act, yet can have a social impact when others cooperate or are influenced to sin by another's actions.

▶ Explain that though sin and evil are present in the world, grace abounds ever more through Christ who is the Redeemer.

▶ Read aloud for the class Ephesians 4:17–32.

Explore

▶ Have students quietly read "Crimes and Sins against Human Sexuality."

▶ Inquire: What methods or groups do you know about in your community, parish or school that help victims of abuse.

▶ Pair students to discuss how demeaning or casual attitudes toward sexuality might lead to overt behavior, criminal acts or grave sin.

▶ Read the Catholics Believe box. Have students discuss how chastity promotes human dignity. Ask them to think about what they could do if someone invites them to engage in inappropriate sexual behavior. They can then reject abusive behavior, move to safety and report it to a trusted adult.

Catholics Believe

Self-mastery as an aspect of chastity takes great effort throughout a person's life and can never be considered fully acquired. Among the sins gravely contrary to chastity are masturbation, fornication, pornography and homosexual practices (CCC 2342–2343).

Crimes and Sins against Human Sexuality

One social evil is the abuse and misuse of human sexuality. When an individual or a group of individuals knowingly chooses to take part in this evil and sins, they degrade the integrity of life and love placed within us. They treat people as "things" to be used for their selfish wants and desires. They violate both the dignity of the person and the image of God, who that person is.

The media often promote and encourage participation in these abuses and misuses of human sexuality. They are sometimes portrayed as doing no harm or even as being glamorous or fun. Cyber bullying, prostitution, pornography, rape and molestation are social evils prevalent in our society today.

 Think about how you can promote the beautiful truth of human dignity.

Cyber-bullying: Cyber-bullying is a type of harassment, which may be sexual in nature. It belittles and threatens violence against someone. Sexual harassment includes the use of offensive language, degrading gestures and extreme sexual stereotyping. Cyber-bullying is no joke, and it should not be treated like one.

Prostitution and Pornography: Prostitution is the practice of buying or selling sexual activity between people. Pornography is any writing, drawing or other imaging with the primary intention of causing sexual excitement. Both prostitution and pornography separate sex from its true place within a loving, committed relationship between husband and wife. Some people who are involved in prostitution and appear in pornography are victims who have been forced into these activities against their will.

Rape: Rape victims are forced to have sexual activity against their will. They do not cause the rape and are never responsible for being raped. Most people who are raped know their attacker. Ninety percent of rape victims are raped by a relative, a friend of the family, someone they date or an acquaintance of some type.

60 Consequences

Teaching Tip

Sexual Abuse Fact Sheet:

• Sexual abuse usually includes inappropriate touching, fondling, prostitution, pornography and obscene phone calls.

• One in four girls and one in six boys will experience some form of sexual abuse before the age of 18.

• Approximately 90 percent of all sexual abuse is done by people the victim knows: friends, acquaintances, family members, teachers, camp counselors, etc.

• Offenders often blame the child for what happens. Children are never to blame for adult abusive behavior.

• There is no typical offender profile. They can be charming, attend church, volunteer in their communities and have families.

Molestation: Molestation is any sexual activity, not limited to sexual intercourse, between an adult and a teen or a child. Like rape, it is a criminal offense in addition to being morally wrong. Any sexual activity between an adult or a minor, and between an older teen and a child, is wrong. It is always sinful. In the first place, the sexual activity is outside of marriage. In the second place, the teen or child cannot legally or morally, give consent to the sexual invitation. It is abuse.

Molesters often seduce their victims so that they will not recognize the sexual activity as wrong. They also make it difficult for the victim to resist by using the sense of respect, fear or shame that the teen or child feels in the presence of the adult or older teen. Molesters also play on the shame, fear or loyalty of the victim to keep them from reporting what has happened to a trusted adult. There is no sin or fault on the victim's part. Yet, they feel ashamed of what has happened to them and want to keep it a secret.

If you are a victim of sexual abuse in any form, speak up. Report it to a parent or other family member, a teacher or another trusted adult. Speaking up and getting help is the very best thing you can do for yourself and everyone involved.

Recognizing these social evils gives us the power to stand up against them. It gives us the power to give witness to the true beauty and purpose of the gift of human sexuality and human love.

Growing in Virtue

Your **informed conscience** can guide you in seeing the social evil of sexual abuse in all forms. Be a conscientious user of the media. Reject messages in the media that degrade a person. Promote only those that respect the dignity of the person.

"A Sign of Sacredness"

In the space provided, sketch an advertisement that promotes the Catholic approach to God's gift of human love as beautiful and sacred.

Consequences   61

Teaching Tip

Sexual Abuse Fact Sheet:

- It is impossible to tell by appearances if a child has been sexually abused. Some appear withdrawn, others are outgoing; some do well in school, others don't. Typically, abuse victims do not interact as well with their peers as other children do. Any remarkable change in a child's typical demeanor or behavior is worth noting. It may not reflect abuse, but it likely reflects some important change that you can help the child negotiate.

- As many as 90 percent of victims never tell anyone about their abuse. It is never too late to tell someone about abuse. Respond with care, comforting authority and effectiveness.

TEACH

▶ Discuss the positive and negative influences of online use (e.g., online social networking can bring friends closer or enable them to use another).

▶ Inquire: What do you think a chaste person would do if they received a sexually explicit e-mail message?

▶ Review with students what they've learned about sexual abuse. Listen closely to their comments; offer corrections as needed. Refer to local diocesan guidelines to shape the limits of this review.

Connect

▶ Read the Growing in Virtue box. Have students privately reflect on how they can use the Internet to promote the important truth of the dignity of each person.

▶ Ask for volunteers to discuss this statement: "There is no harm in posting sexually suggestive words and images online for others to see."

▶ Have students complete the activity on the page. If needed, have them finish the activity at home with their family.

▶ Time permitting, discuss the benefits if their "Sign of Sacredness" was prevalent online instead of the many annoying or negative e-ads.

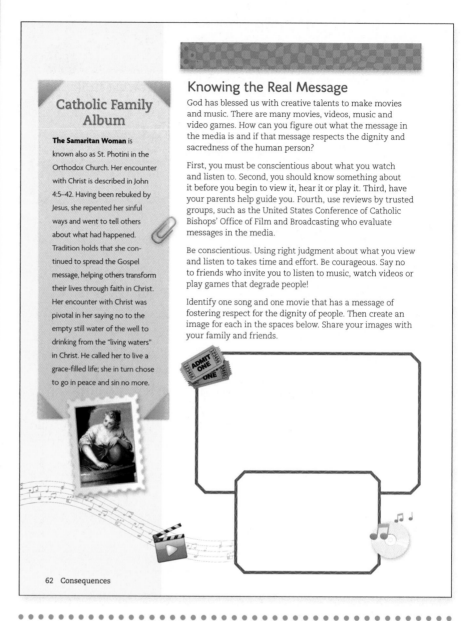

Focus

▶ Have students chart how many hours in a week they spend watching television, listening to music, gaming, using the Internet and the phone.

▶ For each category, have the students summarize what they think they benefit from the time spent on each. Then have them identify some of the main messages being communicated to them via these media.

Discover

Read the Catholic Family Album. Ask: What message did the Samaritan Woman hear from Jesus? *(Repent and believe in the Gospel.)* How did this transform her life? *(She experienced mercy and happiness.)*

Integrate

▶ Read "Knowing the Real Message." Discuss ideas of what the youth do already at home to be an informed user of the media.

▶ Invite students to brainstorm ideas for the activity. Then have students complete the activity on the page.

Pray

Offer a petition that media respect every person.

Catholic Family Album

The Samaritan Woman is known also as St. Photini in the Orthodox Church. Her encounter with Christ is described in John 4:5–42. Having been rebuked by Jesus, she repented her sinful ways and went to tell others about what had happened. Tradition holds that she continued to spread the Gospel message, helping others transform their lives through faith in Christ. Her encounter with Christ was pivotal in her saying no to the empty still water of the well to drinking from the "living waters" in Christ. He called her to live a grace-filled life; she in turn chose to go in peace and sin no more.

Knowing the Real Message

God has blessed us with creative talents to make movies and music. There are many movies, videos, music and video games. How can you figure out what the message in the media is and if that message respects the dignity and sacredness of the human person?

First, you must be conscientious about what you watch and listen to. Second, you should know something about it before you begin to view it, hear it or play it. Third, have your parents help guide you. Fourth, use reviews by trusted groups, such as the United States Conference of Catholic Bishops' Office of Film and Broadcasting who evaluate messages in the media.

Be conscientious. Using right judgment about what you view and listen to takes time and effort. Be courageous. Say no to friends who invite you to listen to music, watch videos or play games that degrade people!

Identify one song and one movie that has a message of fostering respect for the dignity of people. Then create an image for each in the spaces below. Share your images with your family and friends.

62   Consequences

Extending the Lesson

Using Activity Master 9A: Use the Activity Master "What Is Pornography?" This activity examines the differences between pornographic images and other images that honor the human body and or respect the dignity of the human person.

Using Activity Master 9B: Use the Activity Master "Handling Harassment." This activity provides students an opportunity to evaluate the impact of sexual harassment.

Taking a Stand: Encourage the students to communicate their critiques of television programs, movies, online forums and music recordings by having them write a letter. Provide a list of the addresses of major networks, magazine and music publishers, radio stations, etc. Be sure that parents are aware of this activity and give their consent. Encourage parents to help their children in this endeavor since the whole family has the responsibility to be an informed and responsible consumer.

Activity Master 9A

Name

What is Pornography?

Of course you want to learn about your sexuality and your growing and changing body. But does pornography give you honest, accurate information about normal sex? The answer is no! That's not the purpose of pornography.

What are its purposes?

1. First and foremost, to make money for those who produce it. Everyone—producers, actors, and viewers—is demeaned for the sake of profit.
2. To cause sexual excitement in the reader or viewer. Sexual activity is most often distorted or violent in order to make it more dramatic and marketable.
3. To portray people as objects to be used, not as human beings made by a loving God and worthy of respect. *Pornographic sex is always separate from a loving, committed relationship.*

You can use these purposes in judging art, reading material, television, and films. Tell why you think the following materials are pornographic or not.

Michelangelo's statue of David.

A magazine that features nudity.

An anatomy book for art students.

A television show that makes fun of sex.

Family Life Grade 7

© RCL Publishing LLC

Activity Master 9B

Name

Handling Harassment

Sexual harassment is not harmless flirting. It's a show of power. It's a put-down, disguised as playful teasing. Think about harassment and some good ways to handle it.

1. What is sexual harassment?

2. The person who harasses is showing signs of immaturity and insecurity. What do you think he or she gains from embarrassing people in this way?

3. Why shouldn't you put up with this kind of put-down?

4. What reaction from you might discourage a person who is harassing you?

5. When you object to harassment, you might be told that you "asked for it" or that you should be a "good sport." Do you think these are legitimate responses, or is laying blame part of the attack?

6. If the harassment continues over a period of time, what else could you do?

Family Life Grade 7

© RCL Publishing LLC

How to Find It How to Use It

Step 1: Click & Select

Go to RCLBFamilyLife.com
Click on the link for activities.
Then select the activity master you need.

Step 2: Print & Copy

Print each activity master in advance.
Then copy enough for everyone in the class.

Step 3: Share & Discuss

Once students have completed the activity,
have them share and discuss their responses.

LESSON 10 PLANNER

Goal: To explore how individuals contribute to the betterment of society and examine healthy and holy ways to make and maintain friendships

Engage
Page 103

Objective
To explore what it means to live in community

Pray
Prayer of petition

Focus
Read about how manners are at the root of social harmony.

Discover
Team building skills

Teach
Page 104

Objective
To identify polite acts and expressions that build community

Focus
Identify qualities of a good friend.

Explore
Read, discuss and summarize tips for growing in friendship.
Growing in Virtue: Civility and solidarity

Connect
Catholics Believe: The fruits of charity
Illustrate appreciation for friends.

Apply
Page 106

Objective
To discover skills for making and keeping friends

Focus
Analyze and evaluate advice columns.

Discover
Catholic Family Album: Communion of Saints

Integrate
Quiet reflection on giving advice to a friend

Pray
Pray on behalf of a friend.

Reviewing Unit 5
Summarize and review the content from both lessons.

Vocabulary Preview

Civility—the character strength or practice of respectful, polite acts or expressions

Courtesy—a way of acting that shows respect for another person through words and deeds

Forgiveness—the virtue of being able to offer mercy and reconcile with someone who has caused one harm or injury

Manners—socially acceptable behaviors that help people function harmoniously as a community

Social Involvement—a person's participation in the life of a community

Materials Needed

- ▶ writing paper
- ▶ pens, pencils
- ▶ art supplies
- ▶ advice columns
- ▶ Bible
- ▶ Lesson 10 Activity Masters

Call to Prayer

O Most Holy Trinity, you reveal to us what it means to be in communion. You have given to us a special joy in belonging to community. Lead us out of fruitless isolation and help each of us to form and strengthen relational bonds founded on love, respect and generosity. Amen.

Civility

Creating Community

Your first community experiences took place within your family. You learned to express your needs and feelings first in your family. You learned to smile back when someone smiled at you. As you got older, you stepped out into your neighborhood, parish and school. In those larger settings, you learned to relate to different people and various situations. Gradually, you discovered ways to participate in the life of the community. This is called social involvement.

Civility toward one another is basic to living in and building community. Civility includes people being courteous and acting politely, or having good manners toward one another. "Please" and "thank you" were probably the first words of courtesy that you learned. These and other kinds of proper manners are at the root of social harmony and order in cultures all around the world.

For example, in Thailand, people greet one another with "wai." They press their hands together and raise them as if in prayer. In Japan, proper greeting behavior is to bow slightly. French people greet one another with a handshake or a kiss on both cheeks.

Courtesy is a way of acting that shows respect for another person. Courtesy demonstrates social responsibility. When you are courteous to someone and when you treat others with politeness and kindness, you show that you care about how your actions affect others. Your manners also reveal your attitude toward yourself and others. If you have a patient attitude, then you will find it easier to wait for others.

Creating community takes civility. Being civil to one another takes practice and the habit of being courteous and acting with good manners.

> **This lesson will help you to:**
> - **explore** what it means to live in community.
> - **identify** polite acts and expressions that build community.
> - **discover** and use skills for making and keeping friends.

 What are some good manners that you have learned from your family?

Civility   63

Teaching Tip

Words of Kindness: The maxim, "You catch more flies with honey than with vinegar" communicates the truth that we are to use words of kindness instead of words that degrade a person. Some seventh graders will have been victims of demeaning language, or put-downs. These remarks are often tolerated as jokes or just ignored. However, the use of abusive or profane language should never be accepted, tolerated or ignored. Express strong disapproval of such language among your students and expect better of them. Emphasize that they can speak honestly and respectfully without using such language.

ENGAGE

> ### Objective
> To explore what it means to live in community

Pray

Open the lesson with a prayer of petition on behalf of the needs of the local community.

Focus

Read "Creating Community." Allow time for students to make comments or ask questions.

Discover

- ► Place students in groups of four. Provide each group with a supply of gumdrops and toothpicks.
- ► Give them five minutes to assemble, as a group, the tallest structure they can.
- ► Call time, compare structures and discuss the experience.
- ► Ask the groups to analyze their working arrangements, patterns of organization and roles within the group.
- ► Write on the board what the groups identified as skills necessary to work as a team.
- ► Inquire: What are some good manners that you have learned from your family? How do they help create a sense of community?

Objective

To identify polite acts and expressions that build community

Focus

▶ Write on the board: Being a friend means . . . Invite students to complete the statement by adding their own ideas on the board.

▶ Inquire: How have you recently demonstrated these qualities?

Explore

▶ Have students quietly read "Tending to Friends." Then as a class read the text aloud, pausing for students to react or ask questions.

▶ Ask a volunteer to describe how they make friends. Have students re-read the tips for growing in friendship and invite volunteers to share a story from their experience that illustrates one of the tips.

▶ Read the Growing in Virtue box. Discuss the similarities and differences between a community and a friendship.

▶ Define solidarity as the virtue of sharing spiritual and material goods. Explain that solidarity comes from an attitude of equality and respect for each person.

▶ Inquire: How do you and your friends show solidarity?

Growing in Virtue

A community is sustained by civility while friendships are nourished by trust, generosity, forgiveness, honesty loyalty and solidarity. **Solidarity** is the virtue of sharing our material and spiritual blessings out of love for God and others. The practice of solidarity builds true community among people.

Tending to Friends

God looked upon Adam and said, "It is not good for the man to be alone" (Genesis 2:18). In other words, God created us to be social beings. Our desire and need for having friends flows from the fact that God created us to be social beings. Having good friends contributes to our happiness.

Some of what makes two people become friends is a mystery. A sudden or instant friendship can seem remarkable, or "made to be." God guides us in our lives and brings two people together for various reasons, sometimes for a season or sometimes for a lifetime.

Regardless of how friendships begin, they need to be worked on. Friendships need work, effort and attention. Every friendship is of value and needs tending or paying careful attention to. How to make and keep friends are skills everyone needs to learn and practice. A new friendship is like a tiny potted plant. It needs care for it to grow. Without care, a friendship can wither and die due to neglect. Learning how to nourish a friendship will help give it deep roots and allow it to bloom every season.

 Think about the ways you tend to your friends and how you grow friendships.

Here is a list of tips for growing friendships.

- **Be generous.** Friendship involves both giving and receiving. Give of yourself for your friend's sake by listening and being understanding and supportive (see John 15:13).

- **Be forgiving.** There are many ways a friend can hurt your feelings; however, there are more ways to heal. Think twice before you deny your friendship. Always be open to giving and receiving forgiveness (see Sirach 9:10).

- **Be honest.** Do not hide the truth from your friends. Speak the truth in love, even if your friends might not like it (see Sirach 24:26).

64   Civility

Teaching Tip

Thought You Were My Friend: A young person's self-image will often be affected by their ability to make friends. They will often change the way they look and act in order to "fit in" with a group of friends. Help them to understand that a "real" friend will accept them as they are and will not attempt to use them in any way or to buy their affection. Review the concept of "sexual grooming." They should be aware of older children and adults who use flattery, gifts, time together and sharing intimate information or pictures to gain the person's trust and friendship. Offenders may spend months at this before trying anything sexual. Remind students that adults and older teens normally don't try to make friends with younger teens.

- **Be loyal.** Under most circumstances, try to maintain your friendship, even when it is hard to do. A loyal friend does not ignore the wrong a friend does, nor covers it up either. A loyal friend wants what is best and good for their friends (see Proverbs 18:24).
- **Be faithful.** Sticking with your friends during tough times is a good way to grow a friendship. Often this means making sacrifices for them, thinking of their needs before your own. A friendship can grow on the trust between faithful friends (see Proverbs 17:17).

As you grow older, your view of friendship will change. This is the result of your more mature ability to express affection, loyalty, love and forgiveness. The effort you put into building a friendship now will form a foundation for the lasting relationships you will choose when you are an adult. Just as building a community takes civility, friendships are nurtured by civility and more.

Catholics Believe
The fruits of charity are joy, peace and mercy. These are to be found in our friendships. With Christ at the center, friends can be directed by love, grace and freedom (CCC 1829, 1972).

"Homage to Friendship"
Through a visual work of art or the written word, illustrate your appreciation for your friends. Then share your work.

Civility **65**

Student page 65   105

Extending the Lesson

Using Activity Master 10A: Use the Activity Master "Manners." This activity helps students identify specific manners to use in a given situation, a virtual practice if you will. You can also have students role-play these scenarios in front of the class.

A Virtual Friend: Have students imagine that they are trying to make a friend with someone from a different country or culture. This other person knows little about them and the United States of America. Have students write a dialogue using the tips to start the friendship. What would they say? What ideas and experiences would they share? How would they create interest in this other person?

TEACH

Connect

▶ Read the Catholics Believe box. Pair up students to brainstorm the "benefits" of friendship and share how their Catholic faith influences them in forming and living their friendships.

▶ Then have students discuss the importance of honesty and forgiveness between friends. Inquire: What would a relationship be like if there was no trust, no honesty, no generosity, no loyalty, no forgiveness?

▶ Read aloud to the class Sirach 6:5–17. Discuss the connection between the friendships tips and this passage.

▶ Review the concept of "sexual grooming" that has been discussed in previous lessons. How does a sexual predator misuse friendship? Inquire: How can you tell that a person is a true friend and not using friendship as a lure to abuse someone?

▶ Have students complete the activity on the page. If needed, have them finish the activity at home with their family.

▶ Time permitting, discuss how faith in God can strengthen friendships.

Objective

To discover skills for making and keeping friends

Focus

▶ In advance ask students to bring in advice columns they are aware of or read. Tell students that they are going to write their own advice column or letter in this lesson.

▶ Read aloud a few examples in class focusing more on the structure of the writing than on the actual content. Focus also on the tone and style of the writing.

▶ Explain how people seek help and advice from someone whom they believe is an "expert" or has more experience than they do.

Discover

Read the Catholic Family Album. Ask: How is praying to the saints similar to seeking advice on friendship? *(Saints are experts on living the Gospel and the Great Commandment; they can offer spiritual advice through their life stories, as well as through their intercession.)*

Integrate

Read "Friendship and Advice" Provide some quiet time for reflection. Then have students complete the activity on the page.

Pray

Offer a prayer on behalf of a friend in need.

Catholic Family Album

The Communion of Saints includes all the faithful, living and dead who belong to Christ, the Church. The Communion of Saints includes the faithful on earth, those in Purgatory and those in Heaven. Because we live in communion with them, we pray to Mary and all the Saints. We believe that they care for us, their brothers and sisters living on earth.

Friendship and Advice

Here are letters about friendships from other seventh-graders. Imagine that you are writing an advice column. You can refer to the chart on friendship tips to help you out. In the space near each letter, pour out your advice.

Dear Friendship Fixer:
My friend Jason begged to borrow my new denim jacket. At first I said no, because it took me a long time to save up to buy it, and Jason always messes stuff up. He promised to be careful, and I thought he must want to wear the jacket. So I said okay. Jason wore my new jacket to go rock climbing. When he brought it back, it was covered with mud and dust, and there was a big rip in one elbow. All he said was, "Sorry about the rip." I am so angry. What should I do?
Denim Blue in Baton Rouge

Dear Friendship Fixer:
My friend Roberto made the basketball team, but I didn't. All he talks about is basketball. He spends a lot of time at practice. I don't feel like hanging around with Roberto. He said he was mad, and he said it was my fault that we weren't friends anymore. I said it was his. Who's right?
Confused in Colorado

Dear Friendship Fixer:
A girl named Katie recently moved here and started to go to my school. She and my best friend Michelle became best friends. Now they laugh and whisper behind my back. My feelings are hurt. Help!
Stood up in Scranton

66 Civility

Extending the Lesson

Using Activity Master 10B: Use the Activity Master "Wanted: A Friend." This activity helps students expand on the content of the lesson by detailing specific qualities of a friend in need.

Advice Panel: Incorporate some of the advice letters or columns into an advice panel. Using them along with tips for growing a friendship, have a student panel offer advice on how to resolve or address the dilemma mentioned. Change the members of the panel for each dilemma. Have the rest of the class evaluate the advice against the standards established in the tips for growing a friendship. Offer additional standards from Scripture, like Sirach 6:5–17, the Ten Commandments and the Beatitudes.

Activity Master 10A

Name ....

Manners

Did you ever worry about which fork to use, or how to eat spaghetti in public? Good manners aren't all that complicated. You can learn by watching others and thinking about what will make the people around you feel most comfortable. Decide what you might do or say in these cases:

1. You're at a formal dinner party. You're served a strange kind of food you've never had before, and you're not sure whether to eat it with a fork, a spoon, or your fingers.

   _____

2. You're invited to a friend's home for dinner. During the meal, you spill your glass of milk on the tablecloth.

   _____

3. You're getting ready to introduce an old friend to a new one. Suddenly, your mind goes blank. You can't remember your new friend's name.

   _____

4. You're standing at the school door. You see a first grader approach, carrying a large, fragile science project in one arm and some books in the other.

   _____

5. You're making a phone call. When someone answers, you realize you've dialed the wrong number.

   _____

6. You're in a checkout line at a market. The person ahead of you is obviously embarrassed to discover that he doesn't have enough money to pay for his purchases.

   _____

7. You're having trouble understanding someone who doesn't speak your language fluently.

   _____

Family Life Grade 7

© RCL Publishing LLC

Activity Master 10B

Name ....

Wanted: A Friend

Friendship is more than just give-and-take. It requires understanding, sacrifice and honest communication. Complete this two-part exercise and share it with your classmates.

Part One: Write a want ad, telling all the qualities you'd like to have in a friend.

Friend Wanted: _____

_____

_____

_____

_____

_____

_____

Part Two: Now imagine that you're the reader of the want ad. Write a letter telling why you would qualify for the position. Be specific about how you'd be honest, generous, and so on.

_____

_____

_____

_____

_____

_____

_____

_____

_____

_____

_____

Family Life Grade 7

© RCL Publishing LLC

How to Find It
How to Use It

Step 1: Click & Select

Go to RCLBFamilyLife.com
Click on the link for activities.
Then select the activity master you need.

Step 2: Print & Copy

Print each activity master in advance.
Then copy enough for everyone in the class.

Step 3: Share & Discuss

Once students have completed the activity,
have them share and discuss their responses.

Summary

- ▸ Ask the students to read through the Summary section.
- ▸ Invite them to ask questions about any points that are not clear to them.
- ▸ Make sure to expand on any points that were perhaps touched on only lightly during class time.

Thinking It Through

- ▸ Have students answer all three questions on the page.
- ▸ Assign each student a number from one through three.
- ▸ Have students share with the class their answer to the question that corresponds to their assigned number.

Matching It Up

Use this matching section to help the students identify the appropriate definition or description of a key concept, term or person from the unit.

REVIEWING UNIT 5

Name ....

Summary

Remember what you have learned in each of the lessons in God's Gift of Community.

LESSON 9: Consequences

- Personal sins have social consequences
- The social evils of cyber-bullying, pornography, prostitution, rape and molestation are gravely contrary to God's law.
- With an informed conscience, a person can better discern the messages in the media as being healthy and holy or not.

LESSON 10: Civility

- God created us to live in community. Community living depends on each person treating others with respect.
- Friendships are nourished by trust, generosity, forgiveness, honesty and loyalty.
- Through solidarity among friends, we can meet the needs of friendship and build true community.

Thinking It Through

1. How is your school a community and what are some of its unique qualities?

2. What has been most rewarding about your friendships?

3. How does God's love help you contribute to your relationships?

Matching It Up

On each line, write the letter of the description in Column B that best goes with the term in Column A.

 A

1. __C__ Civility

2. __E__ Cyber-bullying

3. __D__ Manners

4. __A__ Sin

5. __B__ Social involvement

 B

A. Deliberate thought, word, deed or omission contrary to God's law

B. A person's participation in the life of a community

C. Character strength of practice of polite acts or expressions

D. Socially acceptable behaviors that help people function harmoniously as a community

E. The misuse of the Internet to degrade or demean others

Unit 5 Review 67

REVIEWING UNIT 5

Name...

Recalling Key Concepts

Circle the T if the statement is true. Circle the F if the statement is false.

1. God made us to live in community. — (T) F
2. Sexual abuse only affects the body. — T (F)
3. Sin is a social act that impacts individuals. — T (F)
4. Showing courtesy is an example of civility. — (T) F
5. Friendships need work, effort and attention. — (T) F

Fill in the missing words in these sentences.

6. **ORIGINAL SIN** was the consequence of the first humans misusing and disobeying God's commandment.

7. When sins such as cyber-bullying and pornography become common in society they are called **SOCIAL** evils.

8. Through the **SACRAMENTS** we receive the graces not to take part in social evils.

9. Praying to and learning about the **SAINTS** is seeking advice on how to love in healthy ways.

10. Friendships are nourished by trust, generosity, forgiveness, honesty and **LOYALTY**.

Working Together

Make a list of online forums that are centered on community living or friendships. Divide into groups, with each group assigned one online forum to evaluate. Create a list of things that the forum provides to build a healthy and holy community based on good friendships. You can create a checklist to share with others or display in school.

Recalling Key Concepts

▶ Use this section to help the students be able to accurately recall the key concepts from the unit.

▶ For the true and false section, you can have students correct any false statements.

▶ To help with the fill-in-the-blank section, you might want to provide a word bank on the board.

Working Together

▶ Choose a project that best fits the need and abilities of your students, as well as your time schedule.

▶ Time permitting, have students complete the unit assessment individually, as a class or at home.

▶ End the unit with a prayer.

Teaching Tip

Empowering Students: Consider using the various questions within the lesson to generate possible thesis statements upon which students can write an essay, journal or report. These thesis statements could also serve as talking points for classroom discussion. The key element is to empower the student to take responsibility for their learning. When they have an active role, such as engaging others in conversation, you might notice their interest is sparked.

Recalling Key Concepts

▶ Use this section to help the students be able to accurately recall important information from the unit.

▶ For the true and false section, you can have students correct any false statements.

▶ To help with the fill-in-the-blank section, you might want to provide the word bank on the board.

Name ....

Recalling Key Concepts

Complete the sentence using one word from the word bank.

PERSPIRATION	FAMILY	LOVE	HORMONES	SACRAMENTS

1. The **FAMILY** .... is your first community.

2. **HORMONES** .... are chemicals that act as messengers throughout the body setting things in motion for the body to grow and mature.

3. **PERSPIRATION** .... when mixed with bacteria can develop an unpleasant body odor.

4. **LOVE** .... is to will the good of another.

5. Through the **SACRAMENTS** ...., we receive the graces not to take part in social evils.

Circle the T if the statement is true. Circle the F if the statement is false.

1. Christian living is shaped by the values of society.   T   (F)

2. Males and females are different in opposite ways.   T   (F)

3. Basic physical health care begins with soap and water.   (T)   F

4. Chastity only applies to those who are not married.   T   (F)

5. Sin is a social act that impacts individuals.   T   (F)

REVIEWING GRADE 7

Name...

Matching It Up

*On each line, write the letter of the description in Column B
that best goes with the term in Column A.*

 A

 B

1. **D** Conjugal love

2. **C** Hygiene

3. **B** Maturity

4. **E** Sin

5. **A** Virtue

A. The habit of acting according to what is moral and good

B. The process whereby one realizes their full potential

C. Practices of cleanliness that promote good health

D. The unique love between husband and wife

E. Deliberate thought, word, deed or omission contrary to God's law

Working Together

In groups write a list of petitions for the whole class to offer in prayer as a way to contribute to the end of this year's learning.

Matching It Up

Use this matching section to help the students be able to identify the appropriate definition or description of a key concept, term or person from the unit.

Working Together

Invite students to form small groups to write their petitions. Give each group time to get organized.

Summary

▶ Ask the students to read through the Summary section.

▶ Invite them to ask questions about any points that are not clear to them. Make sure to expand on any points that were perhaps touched on only lightly during class time.

▶ End the year in prayer with a prayer from The Catholic Home section.

Summary

We have learned about Family Life this year.

God's Gift of Family

- Both the virtue of compassion and the skills of listening help a person communicate effectively.
- Many of your values are formed in your family and these values influence your actions.
- Responsible use of positive peer pressure is a sign of maturity and demonstrates respect for others.

God's Gift of Self

- Spiritual maturity is a lifelong growth process that focuses on living as Christ did.
- God created the human race with two complementary genders, male and female.
- God desires for you to accept and appreciate the gender he created you to be.

God's Gift of Life

- God is the source of beauty and your body reflects divine beauty.
- The Fifth Commandment requires that you take good care of your health.
- Maturity involves making good moral choices for health and life.

God's Gift of Love

- Love is expressed either as friends, neighbors, spouses or unconditionally in imitation of God.
- Sexual attraction is a natural feeling and gift in God's plan for a man and a woman to become husband and wife.
- Chastity integrates God's gift of sexuality within us, respecting each other as persons.

God's Gift of Community

- With an informed conscience, a person can better discern the messages in the media as being healthy and holy or not.
- Friendships are nourished by trust, generosity, forgiveness, honesty and loyalty.
- Through solidarity among friends, we can meet the needs of friendship and build true community.

7

Recognition
of Achievement

The faith community of

_____

proudly announces

_____

and family have completed the seventh level of
RCL Benziger Family Life.

This young person has discovered:
God's gift of family
God's gift of self
God's gift of life
God's gift of love
God's gift of community

May every day provide you and your family new adventures
in following Jesus and in living faithful Christian lives.

_____
(Signed)

This glossary lists and defines the important terms as used in the context of the RCL Benziger *Family Life* program.

abortion: the direct and intentional killing of the human person before birth; direct abortion

abstinence: the avoidance of any sexual behavior or act

abuse: emotional, physical, sexual and/or verbal maltreatment of a person

acceptance: the act of approving or including another through words and actions

acne: pimples on the skin caused by oil clogged pores

addiction: a psychological dependence on something harmful; an unhealthy habit that is difficult to break

adolescence: a stage of life between childhood and adulthood; derived from the Latin, *adolescens*, meaning "growing toward"

adoption: a process where a person or couple legally and permanently care for a child who is not their biological child

adultery: the act of a married person engaging in sexual intercourse with someone who is not their spouse

affection: a feeling of fondness, tender attachment or sign of liking someone, being affected by a person or event

affirmation: the skill of acknowledging the importance of someone through honest praise, which encourages them to do their best

agape: see *charity*; the love of human beings for one another that comes from a love of God

alcohol: an addictive substance found in beer, wine and spirits/liquor

alcoholism: a disease involving a person's addiction to alcohol that harms the person and can result in harming others and often destroys relationships

almsgiving: sharing our blessings with people in need

altruism: the willingness to put the needs of others before one's own

annulment: a decree of nullity granted by the Church stating that the Sacrament of Marriage of a particular couple was invalid

anorexia: an eating disorder of habitually fasting and rigorous exercise based on an obsessive fear of being fat

assisted suicide: helping someone commit suicide

attitude: the ways someone looks at the world and relates to it

attraction: the sense of being drawn to or pulled toward something or someone; in relationships feelings of warmth, trust, care and generosity are experienced

bacteria: tiny, living organisms that can cause decay and other problems in the body

Baptism: Sacrament of Christian Initiation by which a person is joined to Christ, receives the gift of the Holy Spirit and becomes an adopted son or daughter of God the Father and member of the Church

birth order: the sequence of offspring and thus particular position within the family according to when the person was born

blended family: a family formed when adults with children from an earlier marriage enter a new marriage

body: the physical, mortal part of the person that together with the soul forms one unique human nature

budget: a financial tool to aid in managing money

bulimia: an eating disorder in which the person goes through cycles of binging and purging

capital punishment: the right of the government to execute convicted criminals

carbohydrates: a source of energy for the body found in breads, grains, cereals, pasta and rice

celibacy: the state of not being married

cell: the smallest unit of living things

character strength: a good habit that becomes a personal trait enabling one to live virtuously

charism: the grace of the Holy Spirit given to members of the Christian faithful to live out the Christian life in benefit to the Church

charity: the theological virtue of the love a person shows another because of one's love for God, who is the source of such love

chastity: the appropriate and successful integration of the gift of sexuality within the whole person in accord with their vocational state of life

chromosomes: threadlike structures inside each cell's nucleus that contain genes

circulatory system: the system that uses blood to deliver nutrients and oxygen to all parts of the body and pick up cells' waste products

cirrhosis: a disease of the liver that prevents it from removing harmful substances from the blood

civility: see *manners*; the character strength or practice of respectful, polite acts or expressions

cliques: social groups formed to exclude others, often resulting in the harassment of those excluded

common good: the sum total of social conditions which allows people, either as groups or as individuals, to reach their fulfillment more fully and more easily; it presupposes respect for the person

common sense: the ability to know what in general is good and then be able to apply that understanding to a specific situation in order to do the right thing

communication: an exchange of ideas, information, opinions or feelings

community: a group of living things that work together for a common purpose

compassion: the character strength of being able to identify with the situation and feelings of another, built on an attitude of equality

complementarity: to live with and for each other as equal in dignity, helping each other according to God's plan for the two genders

complementary sex: man and woman are not opposites, but complement each other because God created them to be one; also complementary gender

conception: the beginning of human life, the joining of egg and sperm to create new life

confidence: the strong feeling of certitude in oneself through accomplishment or a "can-do" attitude when faced with making a decision

conjugal love: see *spousal love*; the unique expression of sexual love between a husband and a wife who freely give their whole self to each other

conscience: the "inner voice" of a human being from God, within whose heart God's law is inscribed to discern or judge right from wrong, good from evil; a sense of obligation to do what is good and to avoid what is evil

consistent ethic of life: living always with respect for the dignity of the human person

contraception: the mentality and practice of separating the conjugal act from its two purposes of self-giving and life-giving

corporal: relating to or affecting the body

counsel: see *right judgment*; a gift of the Holy Spirit in the ability to make right judgments, to choose what is right and good

courage: see *fortitude*; the strength to do or say what is right and good and to overcome fear, anxiety or any negative attitude that weakens one's confidence to do or say what is right and good

courtesy: a way of acting that shows respect for another person through words and deeds

culture: a way of life passed on through generations shaping people's beliefs, ideas, arts, customs, languages, diet and laws

curiosity: character trait of examining or wondering about someone or something

cyber-bullying: the misuse of the Internet for the purposes of degrading or demeaning others

cytoplasm: the jelly-like fluid inside cells that contains the things a cell needs to live

delayed gratification: satisfaction of reaching an important goal after accepting discipline, sacrifice and inconveniences

dependability: trustworthy, can be relied on

dependence: relying on someone for help and support

depression: a physical or emotional illness that causes persistent sadness and interferes with rational thinking

dignity: inherent value of a human person instilled by God, who created people in his own image and likeness

diligence: in the context of sexual identity, the steadfast attention and appreciation of one's gender

discernment: prayerfully seeking to know God's will individually and personally so that the person's will can align with God's will

discipline: training that helps self-control

divorce: a legal procedure declaring the end of a civil marriage; different from an annulment in the Catholic Church

DNA: the basic ingredient of genes, containing the chemical code that enables genes to guide human growth; also called *deoxyribonucleic acid*

eating disorder: serious, unhealthy eating patterns, behavior or acts

ecology: the science or study of the relationships between living things and the environment

economics: the science or study of dealing with money

economy: the way in which the resources of a country or a community are managed

elderly: older adults, generally older than 70

embryo: the unborn child from the time of implantation in the womb up to the eighth week after conception

emotion: see *feeling*; a state of feeling or subjective experience of a person or event that results in physiological changes or inclines one to act or not act in regard to something felt or imagined to be good or evil

empathy: sensitivity to the needs and feelings of others

encyclical: a letter written by the Pope to be circulated throughout the Church in order to teach important truths at a given time

endangered: in danger of no longer existing, facing possible extinction

endocrine system: a collection of glands that make hormones to regulate body growth, reproductive development and metabolism

environment: the world in which people live, including every living and non-living thing

ethnicity: the particular customs, or ways of doing things, that are handed on from one generation to the next, connected with region, culture or religion

Eucharist: the sacrament of the Body and Blood of Christ

eugenics: the manipulation of human mating and reproduction in order to "enhance" the human race by eliminating certain "undesirable" attributes

euthanasia: the deliberate killing of a person who is elderly, severely disabled or suffering from a serious or terminal illness

extended family: family that includes grandparents, aunts, uncles and cousins

family: two or more people related by blood, marriage or adoption

fecundity: openness to life; the capacity to generate new life

feeling: see *emotion*; a way of responding to something that has happened to the person, inclining one to act in a particular way

fertilization: see *conception*; the beginning of human life, the joining of egg and sperm to create new life

fetus: the developing unborn child from the third month after conception until birth

fidelity: being totally loyal to a person, also known as faithfulness

flowering plants: the largest plant group, including an amazing variety of trees, shrubs, vines, food plants, grasses and weeds

forgive: to reconcile with someone

forgiveness: the virtue of being able to offer acceptance and mercy by reconciling with the person who has caused harm or injury

fornication: sexual intercourse between an unmarried man and unmarried woman; a violation of the Sixth Commandment

fortitude: see *courage*; the cardinal virtue of courage or strength of mind and will to do what is good in the face of adversity or difficulty

foster care: the caring for a child who needs a family for a time

free will: the ability to recognize God as part of our lives and the power to choose between good and evil

gangs: social groups formed around criminal activity, often dealing with vandalism, drugs, robbery or murder

gender: the unique traits associated with being created male or female

generation: a group of related people born around the same time

generosity: the capacity, quality or activity of giving or sharing of oneself or what we have abundantly, beyond basic needs

generous: having an attitude that entails sharing talents, time and money with others

genetic: qualities of living things arising from a common origin and passed from generation to generation through reproduction

gifts of the Holy Spirit: God-given powers and strengths that enable us to work toward the establishment of the Kingdom of God

Gospel: the "good news" of God's mercy and love revealed in the life, Death and Resurrection of Christ

grace: the free and undeserved gift that God gives us to respond to our vocation to become his adopted children; the very life and love of God within us

gratification: having one's needs and or wants met; see *delayed gratification* or *instant gratification*

gratitude: the capacity and ability to choose to be appreciative of all that one receives

grooming: presenting a neat and clean physical appearance

guidance: the help and support people give to others in need

habit: something a person does over and over again, almost without having to think about it

habitat: the place where an animal survives

happiness: a state of contentment or gladness that we must choose to live found ultimately in the love of God

health: the working order of the person as God created and intended them to be; physical health relates to the body while spiritual health relates to the soul, but both are essential to the overall health of the person

Heaven: eternal life with God; being in the presence of God forever; communion of life and love with the Trinity and all the blessed; the state of supreme and definitive happiness, the goal of the deepest longing of humanity

heredity: refers to all traits and characteristics a person inherits from past generations

heterosexuality: sexual attraction to a person of the other or complementary sex

Holy Family: Jesus, Mary and Joseph

homosexuality: sexual attraction to a person of the same sex

honesty: quality or character of being truthful with oneself, others and God

hope: the theological virtue by which a person desires and expects from God both happiness and the grace necessary to attain happiness

hormones: secretions that tell the body how to grow and how to use food; comes from the Greek word that means "to set in motion"

hospitality: accepting others for who they are by offering a welcoming environment

humility: the virtuous ability to be honest about oneself before God and respond to the needs of others when evident

hygiene: practice of cleanliness that promotes good health

identity: the sure knowledge of oneself

imagination: the ability to form a mental image of something that is not present or that does not exist; a gift from God that is a truly human power

implantation: five to seven days after conception, a fertilized ovum leaves the oviduct and attaches itself to the spongy, blood-rich lining of the uterus where it will be nourished until birth

income: money resources of a person, family or group

indissolubility: not able to be dissolved, the quality of permanence

individuality: the quality of being distinguished from others by the ability to think, wonder and choose; unique behavior

infertility: the inability to conceive a child

ingenuity: skills that are creative and used for the benefit of self and others

inspired: to be guided by the Holy Spirit

instant gratification: comforts, pleasures, wants and conveniences being met at the moment

instinct: the ability to carry out an action without having been taught

integrity: being true to the person God created one to be, seeking only what is true, beautiful and good about God, oneself, others and the world

intellect: the part of the mind that thinks, reasons and understands

interdependence: necessary cooperation

intimate: words, experiences or actions shared by those who are close to one another

intoxication: the diminishing effects on the physical or mental abilities to function normally; derived from a Latin word meaning "poisoned"

justice: the cardinal virtue of giving to another what is due to them, what is theirs by right, or ensuring that they have what they need

Kingdom of God: the reign or rule of God; God's saving power and love at work in us

laudableness: praiseworthiness, deserving of one's acknowledgment or reverence

life: the gift from God that allows us to move, grow, think and love

lifecycle: the period for each person from conception until natural death

love: to will the good of another

loyalty: supporting the people in one's life and caring about them

mammals: animals that nurse their young, are warm-blooded, have a backbone and have hair or fur all over their bodies

manners: see *propriety*; socially acceptable behaviors that help people function harmoniously as a community

marriage: a covenantal relationship between a man and a woman in which their spousal love is to be unitive and procreative; Sacrament in which a baptized man and a baptized woman promise love and faithfulness until death

married life: the joining of one man and one woman in the Sacrament of Marriage

mass media: communication intended for the public in various forms, such as print, audio, video and electronic media

maturity: the physical, intellectual, emotional and spiritual growth of the person through which one realizes their full potential appropriate to the person's intellectual or emotional level or age

maxim: a short saying that illustrates or teaches a certain value

mercy: loving kindness toward one who has caused offense in the context of forgiveness and compassion

mind: the part of a person that thinks, knows, learns, remembers and understands

moderation: enjoying things in a balanced and limited way

modesty: the virtue, or practice, of valuing, holding onto and guarding the sacredness of the human body through proper speech, attire and conduct

molestation: unwanted or inappropriate sexual contact

mood: a state of mind at a particular time that moves a person to some kind of action

morality: the goodness or evil of human acts

murder: the direct and intentional killing of an innocent person

muscular system: the system that allows bodily movement

nervous system: the control center of the human body

newborn: the stage in a person's life starting at birth and lasting for about a month

nicotine: an addictive substance that is inhaled in cigarette smoke

non-marital sex: any sexual activity outside the bonds of marriage

nucleus: the control center of a cell

nutrition: the study of foods and how the human body uses them

obedience: to follow willfully the direction, rule or guidance of another person

obligation: the action of committing oneself in service to or benefit for another

obstetrician: doctor specialized in prenatal care, childbirth and postnatal care

occasion of sin: situations that make it more difficult to do what is right and good

organ: body part that directs, or senses information

Original Sin: the first rejection of God's love, which had effects on all human beings

ovary: for plant life, the wide and round part located at the bottom of the pistil that contains seeds

oxygen: a clear, colorless, odorless, tasteless gaseous element produced by plants and needed by animals and people to live

parable: a short simple story told by Jesus to make a point

patience: waiting for something that one needs or wants when one is ready to receive it

peacemaker: one who encourages love and fosters understanding

pediatrician: doctor specialized in the development, care and treatment of children

peer pressure: influence of others upon a person, especially those close to the person, like one's friends

perseverance: the act of continuing with patient effort despite obstacles

personality: the sum total of all the traits and characteristics that express a person distinct from others

perspiration: the production and excretion of moisture from the sweat glands; increases during stress, cooling the body

philia: the affectionate bond of good friends

pistil: the vase-shaped part of a flower that contains the ovaries

pollen: dust-like substances of a flowering plant necessary for plants to reproduce

pollination: the process that prepares the flower to make new life

pornography: any effort to portray real or simulated sexual acts for use by others that betrays the truth and meaning of human sexuality and demeans persons as objects

poverty: a state of seriously lacking in resources or ability to obtain the basic necessities of life usually associated with monetary poverty

pray: the act of listening to and talking with God

pregnancy: nine-month period of development of a human being in the womb of the mother from conception to birth

prejudice: a preconceived adverse opinion or judgment of another

premarital sex: see *non-marital sex*; all sexual activity before marriage thereby violating the dignity of marriage

prenatal: caring for the mother and her child before birth

preteen: the age just before adolescence

pretentiousness: making unjustified or excessive demands, claims or giving greater value to something than warranted or deserved

procreation: participating with God in the creation of new life through sexual intercourse or marital love

profit: the amount of money left over after all the expenses have been subtracted from the income